# A·S·A·P
## AGES, STAGES,
## AND PHASES

# A·S·A·P
# AGES, STAGES, AND PHASES

## FROM INFANCY TO ADOLESCENCE

Integrating Physical, Social, Moral,
Emotional, Intellectual, and
Spiritual Development

## PATRICIA D. FOSARELLI, MD

Liguori
LIGUORI, MISSOURI

*Imprimi Potest:*
Thomas D. Picton, C.Ss.R., Provincial, Denver Province
The Redemptorists

Published by Liguori Publications, Liguori, Missouri
www.liguori.org

**Library of Congress Cataloging-in-Publication Data**

Fosarelli, Patricia D.
 ASAP: ages, stages, and phases of development : from infancy to adolescence : integrating physical, social, moral, emotional, intellectual, and spiritual development / Patricia D. Fosarelli.—1st ed.
  p. cm.
 Includes bibliographical references
 ISBN-10: 0-7648-1501-6 ; ISBN-13: 978-0-7648-1501-0
 1. Church work with children. 2. Child development. I. Title. II. Title: Ages, stages, and phases of development.

BV639.C4.F67 2006
259'.2—dc22                                      2006018499

Liguori Publications, a nonprofit corporation, is an apostolate of the Redemptorists. To learn more about the Redemptorists, visit *Redemptorists.com.*

Printed in the United States of America
10 09 08 07 06   5 4 3 2 1
First edition

# CONTENTS

· · · · · ·

# TODDLERHOOD

# PRESCHOOL YEARS

## EARLY ELEMENTARY SCHOOL YEARS

## PRETEEN YEARS

## YOUNG ADOLESCENTS

## OLDER ADOLESCENTS

# INTRODUCTION
· · · · · ·

S o often, we learn about the various stages of development—physical, social, psychological, and so on—in isolation from one another, as if one did not affect the others.
This lack of integration does not serve our understanding
of the human person who is, indeed, "fearfully and won-
derfully made" (Psalm 139:14). It is difficult to fully understand people by exploring only one aspect of development,
as each aspect influences the others. To know something
about an adult, we need to know something about the child
he or she was. To know something about adult levels of
development, we need to know about levels of development
at younger ages.

And so, this handbook will use a different approach by
taking different ages and looking at their most common
stages of development. The stages of development that will
be highlighted will include physical, psychological (emotional), cognitive, social, moral, and spiritual. Some of these
steps of development can be understood simply by observing many people over time. Other aspects of development
have been observed by theorists who developed their own
theories for development.

As a pediatrician with over twenty-nine years experience,
I am familiar with and able to describe the major, normal,

1

physical developmental milestones at each age. To ensure that every major physical milestone at each age was included, I referred to one of the most consulted pediatric textbooks to verify my experience.

In terms of psychological development, we know much because of the work of Erik Erikson, a psychologist, who explored human development over the life span. Erikson was particularly interested in how people formed relationships with other people and the world. Each of his eight stages consists of something positive versus something negative. At the end of each stage, one has achieved predominantly the positive or the negative, for no one is ever entirely one or the other. In Erikson's view, anyone can remain "stuck" at a certain stage, depending on external circumstances. One can also revisit certain stages later in life, if one did not negotiate them successfully at an earlier age.

We better understand cognitive development in children and adolescents through the work of Jean Piaget, a psychologist who was interested in how children learn. Although Piaget first developed the four stages of his theory by observing his own children, his stages of cognitive development have certainly stood the test of time.

We better comprehend moral development through the work of Lawrence Kohlberg, also a psychologist who theorized six stages of moral development by observing middle-class white boys. His work has been criticized by feminists who believe that women use relational considerations in making moral judgments. It has also been criticized by some minority investigators who believe that their experience is different than that described by Kohlberg. That said, Kohlberg's stages still have value. Although Kohlberg posited six stages, he believed that most people only reached the third or fourth stages.

Finally, we can better appreciate spiritual or faith development through the work of James Fowler, a psychologist and an ordained minister. By observing and interviewing many people, Fowler devised six stages and a "prestage" (for young children). Fowler borrowed heavily from Piaget and Erikson, although in certain stages, one clearly predominates over another.

A summary of the developmental stages posited by Piaget, Erikson, Kohlberg, and Fowler follow.

## Piaget's Stages of Learning

Sensorimotor: birth to two years
Preoperational: three to five years
Concrete operations: five to ten/twelve years
Formal operations: adolescence and adult

## Erikson's Stages of Relationships

Trust vs. mistrust: birth to one year
Autonomy vs. shame and doubt: one to three years
Initiative vs. guilt: three to five years
Industry vs. inferiority: five to ten years
Identity vs. role diffusion: adolescence
Intimacy vs. isolation: young adult
Generativity vs. stagnation: middle age
Integrity vs. despair: old age

## Kohlberg's Stages of Moral Development

Do the right thing (obey a rule) to avoid punishment: preschoolers.

Do the right thing (obey a rule) so that others will think well of one: elementary school-age children.

Do the right thing (obey a rule/law) if it meets one's needs or those of one's family/group, even if it means breaking an external law: adolescence.

Do the right thing (obey a rule/law) to maintain order in one's group or society.

Do the right thing (obey a rule/law) even if it is not one's own if breaking it would cause embarrassment or hard feelings.

Universal principles take precedence over any local rule; obey universal principle, even if it means losing one's life to do so.

## Fowler's Stages of Faith

Undifferentiated faith: birth to two years
Intuitive-projective faith: three to five years
Mythic-literal faith: five to ten years
Synthetic-conventional faith: preteens and young adolescents
Individuative-reflective: older adolescents and young adults
Conjunctive faith: middle age (if ever)
Universalizing faith: middle age and beyond (if ever)

We will explore these stages, age by age. Also highlighted will be each age's "phases," those little quirks that human beings experience at one age more than at others. Although some of these phases seem completely irrational, knowledge of the other changes going on at the individual's age helps to make better sense of them.

Also included throughout each chapter are verses in the form of haiku, a Japanese style of poetry. These three-line poems consist of five syllables in the first line, seven in the second, and five in the third. The purpose of these haiku is to highlight the various stages or phases in a pithy, sometimes humorous, manner so that they might be better understood and remembered.

The goal of this handbook is to help all who use it better understand the development of children from birth through adolescence so that we can minister more effectively to them and, perhaps also, to their families. If we who work with children and adolescents understand their stages of development well, we can share that knowledge with parents and others who work with young people in a variety of settings.

# INFANCY

· · · · · ·

*Crying lustily—*
*Newborn baby sees the light,*
*tightly shuts her eyes.*

· · ·

*Far too premature!*
*Struggling (hard) to breathe alone*
*So much work to live.*

Most of us do not teach infants and toddlers, unless they are our own. Nevertheless, to understand preschoolers, it is important to understand how babies and toddlers develop. Because babies and toddlers are, for the most part, preverbal, there is not a lot to say about certain stages (for example, moral), but a great deal to say about other stages (for example, physical).

The following two chapters are a brief overview of the development of infants and toddlers, children younger than thirty to thirty-six months.

## Physical Development—Gross Motor

*Kicking infant coos*
*at plain, unpainted ceiling,*
*whatever is there?*

*Rotating himself*
*onto his belly, change of*
*perspective profound!*

The newborn infant can do very little on his own and must rely on others to meet his every need. He must be fed, changed, and bathed. If he is crying, it is up to the adult to determine the cause and rectify it. Newborns with normal hearing will startle at a loud noise by crying and extending their arms and legs. Contrary to common belief, newborns can see, well enough to imitate the facial expressions of those interacting with them. Because their muscles are not yet well developed, newborns have poor head control. They cannot keep their heads upright and need those holding them to support their necks. Careless or rough handling of such a young infant can cause a serious injury. Seemingly constantly hungry, the newborn will root at anything that resembles a chest—male or female—in an attempt to find milk. He might also suck vigorously on his hands.

As the months go by, an infant's muscles strengthen, and his nervous system matures. He still hears well, but loses the characteristic startle reflex at loud sounds. His vision generally becomes sharper, and he can spend hours staring at mobiles or other toys. Eventually, he will be able to lift his hands up in front of his face and gaze intently at them. At several months of age, he will begin to roll over—first from front to back (three to four months), then from back to front (four to five months).

Once head control and rolling are mastered, the infant will be able to scoot around in his crib or playpen. Such scooting is the precursor of creeping and crawling, which occur in the latter part of the first year of life. He will also be able to sit, initially only for a few seconds and with much support. Later, when his neck and truncal muscles are strong, he will sit alone without support (around six months). While sitting, he might support himself by placing one hand between his legs to steady himself. This is called "tripoding" and begins at around five months. Once sitting without support is mastered, he will be able to reach for an object without falling over.

In addition, once independent sitting is mastered, an infant will try to pull himself to standing. Usually, this is first done in a crib or playpen and occurs at seven to eight months. The infant needs the support of something to hold onto. Otherwise, he will fall. Eventually, when standing in place becomes routine, many infants try to cruise, to move sideways holding onto an object, such as a sofa. This typically occurs at eight to nine months. Shortly thereafter, an infant usually begins to walk, first by holding onto (tightly!) the hands of parents and then later on his own. Walking officially turns an infant into a toddler. Most infants begin to walk independently by nine to twelve months.

Infants can also get around by creeping (that is, pulling oneself along) and crawling (that is, synchronized right-left arm and leg motions) across a floor or other surface. Creeping usually first appears between six to seven months, and crawling at seven to eight months. Many infants continue to crawl even when they can walk because they are so good at it. Never underestimate the speed of an experienced crawler!

## Physical Development—Fine Motor

*Five stubby objects*
*moving as if by magic—*
*Baby finds his hand.*

• • •

*Pudding for dessert*
*eatable and squishable*
*between wee fingers.*

The newborn infant's movements seem almost purposeless (even though they aren't), because coordination is lacking. Most of the time, the newborn's hands are fisted. Fisting will remain the norm until about three to four months. As the weeks go by, the infant will begin to occasionally open his hands and eventually grasp objects with some purpose, such as wanting to grab a parent's finger or touch other objects like a bottle. At four months, an infant is able to manipulate his fingers. By the time that an infant is able to lay on his belly and hold his head up, he will also attempt to "bat" objects within his line of vision with his hand. At around five months of age, he will begin to transfer objects from one hand to another and pull objects toward himself (usually with a laugh). Eventually, after six months of age, he will "rake" objects toward him in a manner similar to raking leaves. As his muscles and nervous system mature, he will increasingly be able to try to pick up small objects, and pull (hard!) at others. By nine months, if an object is dropped onto the floor from a height, an infant will look down (or over the edge) to find it.

Because "raking" is quite inefficient in picking up objects of interest, most infants will develop what is called a "scissors" grasp by nine months; this looks like the infant is holding an imaginary pair of scissors. That, too, is inefficient, and by ten to twelve months, an infant will develop a "pincer grasp," bringing his thumb and index finger together to pick up small objects. This includes toys, food, glasses, and other items. Many of these objects will land in his mouth, regardless of whether they constitute food or not! Infants can place an object in a cup and "dump" it out by ten to twelve months. A favorite game is to hide an object under a cloth, cup, box, and then find it. His facial expression demonstrates his sense of accomplishment!

Mealtimes will become quite lively, as infants handle each food item with their hands, sometimes throwing or dropping food and watching it hit the floor! At this age, many infants will insist on holding their own bottles. Some will be able to drink neatly from a cup, although others will do so sloppily, if at all. Children vary in their abilities to use a spoon, some not until well into the second year of life.

## Physical Development—
## Sleep, Diet, and Elimination

Most newborns infants sleep up to twenty hours each day. As they mature across the first year of life, the amount of sleep gradually decreases, so that by twelve months of age, an infant sleeps twelve to fifteen hours each twenty-four-hour period. This includes nights and naps. Most infants achieve a full-night sleep, without awakening, sometimes in their first year of life. Those who continue to awaken at night frequently do so because they want the company of a parent.

Infants can grow well on breast milk or formula alone in the first year of life, and, in some cultures, that is an infant's normal diet. In our culture, cereal is added at four to six months, with fruits and vegetables soon after. Meats are usually not offered until well into the second half of the first year of life. These foods should all be eaten with a spoon (as opposed to placing cereal in a bottle) for otherwise normal children. See the last paragraph under "Physical Development—Fine Motor" for more information on a child's ability to feed herself.

Newborn infants can wet their diapers ten to twelve times each day. This decreases over the first year of life. In addition, newborn infants can stool in their diapers multiple times each day—sometimes after every feeding! By the end of the first year of life, the frequency generally decreases to one to two bowel movements each day, although some infants have a normal pattern of one every other day.

## Psychological/Emotional Development

*Mobile above crib*
*all day round and round turning*
*baby mesmerized.*

• • •

*Enjoys making noise—*
*squeals and screeches without end*
*just to hear himself.*

Because infants cannot speak, it's hard to know what is bothering them. Infants communicate by crying, and all parents learn that different cries have different meanings, such as the "hungry" cry is not the same as the "hold me" cry. Some infants have temperaments that are very easy. They cry and fuss very little and seem happy no matter what the conditions. Other infants have difficult temperaments. Nothing seems to satisfy them, and if one need is satisfied, another surfaces. Some infants grow out of their difficult temperaments, while others do not.

Although infants can be alert to sounds by becoming quiet or startling by one month, they truly smile responsively at four to six weeks and laugh by three to four months. Some infants have real belly laughs! What makes a baby laugh is sometimes a mystery, for many babies laugh to themselves when they are alone.

Around three months or so, infants coo at both animate and inanimate objects. If their hearing is good, they can also orient to a voice by looking toward it. Initially, that look will be fleeting, but as time goes by, it will become more persistent. At around five months of age, an infant can make a "raspberry" (albeit with a lot of drooling!) and say "ah, goo." After six months of age, infants babble, which is repetitive consonant sounds, such as "ba, ba, ba" or "da, da, da." (As an aside, this is why parents think that their child is intentionally saying "da-da" for daddy.) Infants will babble at anyone or anything, and their use of sounds is not done specifically.

An infant's first word is usually "da-da," because it is an easy sound for him to make; "ba-ba" or "ta-ta" might follow soon after. These sounds are not used specifically. "Ma-ma" and "bye-bye" come a little later, because they are harder for the infant to articulate. Specific use of "da-da" or "ma-ma" occurs at nine to twelve months. By the end of the first year of life, an infant has about two words. Some infants might have up to four.

Psychologist Erik Erikson looked at the psychological stages throughout the human life span. Germane to infants is the first stage. *Trust vs. mistrust* (birth to twelve months) means that if an infant does not receive trustworthy care when she is most vulnerable, she learns not to trust. This mistrust includes not only those who have treated her badly, but also others. To her, the world is not a trustworthy place.

## Cognitive Development

*Ho-hum afternoon,*
*baby giggles for first time—*
*now momentous day.*

• • •

*Crawling on the floor,*
*electric outlet looms large—*
*small fingers explore.*

Jean Piaget was interested in how children learn about their world. The infant-toddler stage is called *sensorimotor*. Infants and toddlers learn about the world by using their senses and placing objects in their mouths. When they are able to be independently mobile, they can move toward the objects that they want to explore rather than having to wait for others to bring them.

Admittedly, it is hard to know exactly what young infants know since they cannot speak and their ability to respond is limited. By six months of age, however, it is clear that an infant's ability to understand is far more developed than the ability to speak. For example, if one says to a seven-month-old, "Look at Daddy," it is likely that the infant will do so. This ability to comprehend matures over time. In fact, by the end of the first year of life, many infants will be able to easily follow one-step commands, such as "Give your ball to Mommy." This is especially likely if the command is accompanied by a gesture. It will be many, many months before the same child will be able to repeat such a command and even longer before she will be able to speak one on her own. As was stated earlier, by the end of the first year of life, an infant has about two to four words. By the end of the second year, that will jump to fifty.

## Social Development

*Infant delighted—*
*squeals in appreciation—*
*a new human face!*

• • •

*Wearing her dinner*
*like ladies wear fine jewelry*
*she grins for pictures.*

Young infants do not mind being held by anyone who is gentle, and they will smile at anyone who smiles at them. By the second half of the first year, many infants show fear of strangers or fear of being separated from her parents, especially the mother. "Strangers" might not be strangers at all; they might be relatives! These behaviors might continue well past the child's second birthday. (See "Major Phases Beginning in Infancy.") With those whom the infant or child feels comfortable, she will enjoy games of "peekaboo," hiding and finding objects, and imitating funny sounds.

## Moral Development

*"No-No," from mommy*
*his face erupt in sobs—*
*unfairness of life.*

• • •

*Tone of daddy's voice*
*stops him in his tiny tracks—*
*hating these moments.*

Infants do not have the developed moral sense of their older siblings. After about six months of age or so, infants can recognize displeasure in an adult's voice. By the latter part of the first year of life, hearing "no-no" causes most infants to stop what they are doing (at least temporarily!) and look at the person saying the words. "No-no" in a firm voice can actually stop a child from doing what she is doing at any age if she believes that there will be consequences to her actions.

## Spiritual Development

*Jabbering away*
*to someone nobody sees—*
*could someone be God?*

• • •

*Folding tiny hands*
*just like mommy and daddy—*
*dinner on the way.*

Although most adults think that infants must be closer to God than they are because infants cannot turn away from God, it is not clear what is the content of the spiritual lives of infants. Nevertheless, older infants can fold their hands in prayer before meals or at bedtime if they see their parents do so. James Fowler, a psychologist and a minister, noted stages of faith development across the life span. He called the stage during infancy and toddlerhood a pre-stage: *undifferentiated faith*, meaning that if children trust those around them, they will have faith in them. If those individuals speak about God lovingly and reverently, the children will learn to have the same ideas about God. On the other hand, if the individuals speak of God in irreverent or sloppy language, children will learn to do the same. If the individuals ignore God altogether, so will the children.

# Major Phases Beginning in Infancy

### *Separation anxiety*
*Eyes filled with horror—*
*Mommy walking across room*
*leaving him alone.*

Around six months of age, an infant seems to be terrified of being separated from her primary caretaker(s), usually the mother. If someone picks her up, the infant will look worriedly for her parent. She might also cry (lustily!) and hold her arms out. This behavior occurs even with people with whom the infant has previously been comfortable. Some infants even exhibit this behavior with their fathers, crying inconsolably when their fathers carry them away from their mothers. Separation anxiety can occur even when an infant's mother (or other primary caregiver) is in full view.

Separation anxiety is related to the fact that the infant's memory is developing, and she remembers how important her primary caregiver is to her. Because she does not have much experience, she cannot be certain that she will ever see this person again. Thus, she behaves as if her whole world were falling apart and that she will be abandoned.

Separation anxiety lasts until about thirty months of age. Adults do well to respect a child and not force him to be held by anyone he does not seem to know or like.

### Stranger anxiety
*Not in the least bit
interested in new face—
'cuz not mom or dad.*

When an infant is experiencing stranger anxiety, which also occurs at about six months of age, she becomes very afraid of strange or unfamiliar people. This might include relatives she does not see very often. This, too, is related to the infant's growing memory and sense of safety around only certain people.

Stranger anxiety lasts until about thirty months of age. Again, adults do well to respect a child and not force him to be held by anyone he does not seem to know or like.

### Playing with food
*Spaghetti a mess
when on floor, in hair, on wall—
new parents in shock.*

Because infants love to explore everything with their hands, they carry this love to their meals. Parents are sometimes dismayed that their eight-month-old feels the need to play with her food before she begins to eat it or throws it on the floor. Playing with her food is one way an infant learns about different textures. Many infants carry this behavior well into their second year of life. Adults do well to "go with the flow" in infancy by putting paper or plastic sheeting under an infant's highchair at mealtimes to facilitate the cleanup.

*Night waking*
*Far into the night*
*infant considers it day,*
*cooing and playing.*

Many infants sleep through the night for several months, and, then, without warning, wake up crying in the middle of the night. When a parent arrives to console such an infant, his tears cease. Maybe even a little playtime occurs. When the infant sees that he can get a parent's full attention in this way, if he awakens again in the middle of the night, he will cry out again...and again. A habit becomes established, one that is particularly hard to break. As long as night waking is in an infant's best interests, he will continue to do it. After all, he can catch up on *his* sleep in the day!

Some infants who night-wake scream—for what seems like hours—until someone comes to them. Then, almost by magic, the crying and screaming stop. When the parent leaves the room, or even tries to leave, the oral outburst begins anew.

Night waking can start in the second half of the first year of life and continue through the entire second year. It is best handled by checking the child to ensure that nothing is wrong with him, but doing so in his crib. He is not to be held or carried about, because that is what he wants. That does not mean a parent has to be mean—far from it! A parent should gently talk to his child by standing at the side of the crib. He certainly can (and should) touch him. But, he should not lift him out of the crib unless there is a very good reason to do so. When the parent feels it is time

20

to leave, he should do so, even if the child begins to cry again. This is difficult but necessary if a child is to learn to sleep by himself all night. The incidence of night waking is less in those children who fall asleep in their cribs and not on the sofa or playpen, because infants then associate the crib with sleep.

## Summary • Questions • Resources

What a miracle God has given us in the first year of life! At the beginning of that year, the infant is completely helpless, unable to even turn over or lift his head. Sleeping most of the day, his waking hours are mostly taken up with feeding. By the end of that year, he will be able to walk independently, say a few words, understand some simple commands (including "no-no"), and know enough about his world to be delighted with certain people and things but afraid of other people and things. No longer just a baby like other babies, he clearly has his own personality that can be shaped by the words and actions of those around him. What a magnificent miracle the conception, birth, and development of a new human being is. How awestruck we all should be.

## Questions—Catechists

- What kind of advice do you give to a parent whose young infant is crying lustily in church? What do you say to other parishioners who complain about the crying?

- What kind of advice could you give to the parents of a six-month-old during baptismal preparation when they mention that they are afraid that their infant will cry at the sight of the pastor because she is afraid of strangers?

- What advice can you give parents about spiritual practices that they might initiate with an infant?

## Questions—Parents

- What would you do if your infant cried loudly throughout a church service?

- What might you do if your child is very afraid of strangers or of being separated from you and people at church want to hold your infant?

- Do you think that praying with your infant makes any sense? What about bringing him to church regularly?

## Resources

Erikson, Erik: *Childhood and Society.* New York: WW Norton & Co., 1985 [especially chapter 7].

Fowler, James: *Stages of Faith: The Psychology of Human Development and the Quest for Meaning.* San Francisco: HarperSanFrancisco, 1995 [especially chapter 15].

McMillan Julia, Catherine DeAngelis, Ralph Feigin, and Joseph Worshaw (eds): *Oski's Pediatrics: Principles and Practices, Third Edition.* Philadelphia: Lippincott Williams & Wilkins, 1999 [especially tables 119–1; 119–2; 120–1; 120–2; 395–1].

Shelov, Steven (ed): *(The American Academy of Pediatrics) Caring for Your Baby and Young Child, Birth to Age 5.* New York: Bantam Books, 1991. [Excellent reference book.]

Siberry, George, and Robert Iannone (eds): *The Harriet Lane Handbook.* St. Louis: Mosby, 2000 [especially chapter 9].

Singer, Dorothy, and Tracey Revenson: *A Piaget Primer: How a Child Thinks.* New York: New American Library, 1978 [especially chapter 2].

# TODDLERHOOD

· · · · · ·

*Teething such a pain—*
*All this to eat solid foods?*
*Milk looking better.*

• • •

*First step the hardest—*
*Will the floor hold or open,*
*swallowing him up?*

The toddler years are a wonderful time when the once-helpless infant becomes more independent and steadily develops in a number of areas. Language is acquired, mobility is achieved, and a young personality becomes even more obvious. It is also the time for battles as the child must get used to the fact that he cannot do whatever he wishes and that, even if he can do it, his parents might prevent it.

## Physical Development—Gross Motor

*Standing on tiptoes*
*her mouth formed into an "O,"*
*she meets butterflies.*

*Kitty in uproar!*
*Toddler yanking tail too hard,*
*thinks he's being nice.*

In the second year of life, toddlers' gross motor skills continue to improve. Walking becomes routine and running becomes the challenge…and eventually the norm! Toddlers can walk backward at fourteen to fifteen months of age, and they learn to run at about the same time. Toddlers love to jump up and down. They also love to climb. Opening drawers, cabinets, and doors becomes a game. Toward the end of the second year, toddlers become quite proficient at mimicking what adults are doing, whether that's sweeping the floor or hammering a nail. The greater mobility of toddlers (and their complete lack of understanding of dangers) makes it imperative that rooms that they occupy—even for a *brief* time are "childproofed." It takes only a few seconds for a child to stick her fingers in an electric outlet, burn herself on a hot light bulb, or to swallow pills or a cleaning solution.

## Physical Development—Fine Motor

*Two-year-old struggles*
*to stab tiny peas with fork—*
*they keep escaping.*

• • •

*Working intently*
*to place a pea in her nose—*
*just because it's there.*

As the second year of life begins, many toddlers must be watched carefully to ensure that they do not put themselves in harm's way by ingesting poisons or nonedible objects, placing their fingers in electric outlets, touching hot objects, and so on. Children of this age might attempt to dress themselves, albeit in a very rudimentary fashion. Naturally, they make many mistakes.

Children in the second year of life attempt to color and draw. Their efforts should not be judged by adult standards. A toddler can make simple marks with a crayon by twelve to thirteen months, imitate a scribble by fifteen to sixteen months, and spontaneously scribble at about eighteen months. He will not be able to imitate a vertical or horizontal line until well over twenty-four months of age.

Toddlers also play with dolls or other toys that require their interaction. For example, they love playing with blocks and can make a tower of three blocks by eighteen months. Their play frequently imitates what they see in those around them. Good toys are those that are brightly colored and able to encourage both learning and fun.

## Physical Development—
## Sleep, Diet, and Elimination

Most toddlers sleep ten to twelve hours each day (nights and naps). Some toddlers still do not sleep through the night...much to their parents' dismay! Although there might be a medical reason for night waking, the most common reason is wanting the parents' attention.

Toddlers are quite messy eaters and enjoy playing with

their food. Yet, they are gradually becoming more adept at using a spoon. Like all human beings, toddlers have food preferences and can be picky eaters, sometimes "holding out" for the foods they most want. In general, vegetables are not preferred foods, while sugary foods are. That is why it is a good idea to limit a toddler's intake of sugary foods (including soda) and fatty or salty foods, because taste preferences for a lifetime can be established as early as the second year of life. Food portions need to be small to avoid both waste and overwhelming the toddler. After all, he can always get another serving if he so desires.

Toddlerhood is the time when most children are toilet trained (twenty-four to thirty months). Most toddlers urinate four to six times each day and have a bowel movement once each day, although some toddlers have one every other day.

## Psychological/Emotional Development

*Dwarfed by a huge world,*
*she hugs herself, sucking thumb,*
*mouthing, "Momma, come."*

• • •

*First snowflake landed*
*right on her nose. How dare it?*
*Alas! Twas all gone.*

In addition to actual words, toddlers use "jargoning," which sounds like they are speaking in a foreign language since they are using inflections of voice. Even as they are increasing in their ability to say "real" words throughout the second year of life, they are imitating, through jargoning, and the voice inflections, facial expressions, and body language of those around them. This is a very important step in language development. Parents who speak in angry tones frequently have toddlers who do the same. Parents who speak calmly are more likely to have toddlers who do the same.

As toddlers gain more independence in the second year, they will increasingly make their wants known, with gestures, words, or jargoning. They can be quite stubborn, and this is a normal stage. They can also be clingy, especially if they are tired or feel threatened. Usually, they are energetic and happy. Yet, fears can occur, especially of loud, large objects such as a flushing toilet. (See the section below on "Major Phases Beginning in Toddlerhood.")

In psychologist Erik Erikson's stages of building relationships, the next stage is applicable to toddlers. *Autonomy vs. shame/doubt* (twelve to thirty-six months): if a toddler is not allowed to become more independent and to do things on her own, she might doubt her abilities or be ashamed of her inadequacies. This is especially true if significant adults shame her when she fails. Thus, she might resist trying new things, limiting her development. This stage is highlighted by toilet-training battles. (See "Major Phases Beginning in Toddlerhood.")

## Cognitive Development

*Look of confusion—*
*computer keyboard looms large*
*to tot. Not for long.*

• • •

*Ruckus in back pew—*
*banging Tonka truck throughout*
*pastor's long sermon.*

In the second year of life, children improve their ability to speak and like to imitate words, as mentioned in the "Psychological/Emotional Development" section. By fourteen to sixteen months, they can follow a one-step command without any gestures from the parent, and by twenty-four months, a two-step command can be followed. By eighteen to twenty-four months, a toddler will be able to identify several body parts if he has been taught them. Many toddlers may know more than six to eight body parts.

By thirty months, a child will understand pronouns and what "one" means, as in "You can only eat one cookie." By thirty-six months, a child will have a vocabulary of 250 to 300 words and can easily compose a three-word sentence (up from twenty-four months when he could only compose a two-word sentence). Children who are thirty-six months old can generally name at least one color, use personal pronouns appropriately, and understand at least two preposition commands. The latter means that a child knows, for example, that "Put the book *on* the shelf" is not the same as "Put the book *under* the shelf."

Toddlers like to try new things that they have seen others do. This can be a good thing or a bad thing, depending on what is being imitated! Also, at this age, if one is reading to a child, she will indicate to the reader what she would like to have read. Toddlers love to point! Books with lots of pictures are very popular at this age, and toddlers will point to certain pictures. If the reader names the picture, many toddlers will try to repeat the word, especially after eighteen months of age. One should always say the name of the object to which a toddler is pointing to assist in her language development.

## Social Development

*First time in ocean—*
*he splashes wildly above*
*dad's safety-net arms.*

\* \* \*

*Playing well alone*
*til sibling appears—squabble!*
*Inevitable.*

In the second year, the toddler will still enjoy the games mentioned above, but will also enjoy other kinds of games such as the more physical ones. By the time a child is three years old, she can play simple games with another—but the rules of the game might be quite loose!

## Moral Development

*Sitting in time out*
*she broods, plotting what she'll do*
*when she's all grownup.*

• • •

*Written all over*
*his face—the stolen cookie*
*he poorly conceals.*

Like infants, toddlers do not have the better developed moral sense of their older siblings. A toddler can easily recognize displeasure in an adult's voice. Hearing "No-no" causes most toddlers to stop what they are doing (at least temporarily!) and look at the person saying the words. "No-no" in a firm voice can actually stop a child from doing what she is doing at any age if she believes that there will be consequences to her actions. The earliest stage of moral development that Lawrence Kohlberg noted was doing the right thing because of fear of punishment. Like the next age group (preschoolers), toddlers do what is right (or don't do what is wrong) because they do not want to be punished, whether the punishment is a deprivation of something wanted, a timeout, a verbal reprimand, and so forth. This is normal for this age.

## Spiritual Development

*Tightly shutting eyes—*
*"God is great, and God is good,"*
*he prepares to eat.*

•  •  •

*Is God really there*
*in bedrooms darker than night?*
*Toddler hugs teddy.*

James Fowler felt that infants and toddlers share the same stage in faith. He called the stage during infancy and toddlerhood a pre-stage: *undifferentiated faith,* meaning that if children trust those around them, they will have faith in them. If those individuals speak about God lovingly and reverently, the children will learn to have the same ideas about God. On the other hand, if the individuals speak of God in irreverent or sloppy language, children will learn to do the same. If the individuals ignore God altogether, so will the children.

Although most adults think that infants and toddlers must be closer to God than they are because of their inability to turn away from God, it is not clear what the content of the spiritual lives of infants and toddlers actually *is* because they cannot talk about them. Nevertheless, toddlers will fold their hands in prayer before meals or at bedtime if they see their parents do so. Toddlers might even be able to say very simple prayers, especially by their second birthday.

## Major Phases Beginning in Toddlerhood

*Temper tantrums*
*Kicking and screaming,*
*banging her head, all because*
*"no" was the answer.*

With a child's growing independence and a desire for autonomy, the onset of temper tantrums is almost inevitable. After all, a toddler does not really understand the future. Saying, "In five minutes" to her has as much meaning as communicating to her in a foreign language. So, when she wants something, she wants it now! When she wants to do something, she wants to do it now! Naturally, reality sets in: she cannot get what she wants. She is not able to do what she wants, not only because someone wouldn't let her do it but also because she is not physically capable of doing it. Her frustration erupts into an outburst. This outburst has a variety of forms, but usually each child has her own style in temper tantrums. Crying loudly or screaming is generally part of every tantrum, accompanied by associated behaviors. Some children stomp their feet; some lie down and kick; some throw things; some try to knock things over.

While all these behaviors are, unfortunately, in the realm of "normal" at this age, biting and hitting are not and should not be permitted.

The best way to handle these outbursts is to ignore them or to direct a child's attention to something else. Although a child's first few temper tantrums might be his own reactions to his limitations, if parents or others respond to the child by giving him what he wants, future tantrums will be a mixture of the child's frustration and his hope that such behavior will reward him with that which he most wants. (As an aside, we know this because when a child in the midst of a ferocious temper tantrum and is given what he wants, he stops—*immediately*.)

Depending on how parents and others close to the child handle these outbursts, they might be mild and very short-lived, or they might be very "showy" and last well into the preschool years.

### Fears

*Flushing toilet roars,*
*threatening his very life.*
*Diapers aren't so bad.*

As the toddler begins to realize that there is a big world out there and that he is quite small, he begins to have fears. Many normal fears include: fear of the toilet (because it's loud and noisy), fear of going down the bathtub drain (because if water can go down, why can't he?), fear of the dark (because who knows what's really there when one can't see?), fear of animals (especially if he was bitten or scratched by one), fear of bugs, and some idiosyncratic fears (for example, fear of clowns, fear of a certain color). Are many of these fears irrational? Yes, but who expects a toddler to be rational?

Fears that have a grounding in reality usually last longer than fears that do not. For example, a child who was bitten by a dog might have a lifelong fear of dogs (or at least ones that look like the dog that bit him), while a child who seems afraid of dogs might lose that fear when the family gets a playful puppy.

Adults do well to treat a child's fears gently and respectfully. Trying to embarrass a child out of his fear is usually counterproductive. Instead, a soothing voice and a calm explanation of why the danger is not so bad get most children through their fears by the preschool years (although new fears might arise at anytime in life—even in adulthood).

*Transitional objects*
*(AKA "security blankets")*
*Such angst and drama!*
*A major catastrophe!*
*Blankie being washed.*

At this age, many young children have an object that they can hold (or even clutch) when they are tired, frustrated, or fearful. The identity of the object is important to the child, and usually there is only one such object for a particular child. Common transitional objects include a treasured doll or stuffed animal, a blanket, or a piece of a parent's clothing. Attempts to take it away—either temporarily to wash it or permanently—are usually met with strong objections! No toddler should be ridiculed for dragging around such an object, no matter how soiled or torn it is.

A transitional object is a toddler's way to comfort himself in times of stress. As he becomes older, he will learn to comfort himself internally, although many adults use external means to deal with stress, such as smoking and chewing gum. Transitional objects can last into the early preschool years, especially if the child has never been away from his parents before.

### Food "jags"/food refusals
*Hot dogs and hot dogs—*
*all he eats, going on weeks.*
*Mom panic-stricken.*

Some toddlers get on a food jag: they will only eat a certain food and nothing else. Parents, concerned that their child will starve, give in to these jags. As a result, a child gets what she most wants: she doesn't have to eat the "yukky" food, but only the food she really likes. It should be said from the outset that few children (if any) get food jags over vegetables! Generally, the food of interest is of the "junk" variety or is very starchy, such as spaghetti. When in a food jag, a child will insist on the same food for every meal.

This is best handled by offering a child a variety of foods and *not* caving in to the food jag. No child has ever starved to death because he could not have spaghetti or chocolate for every meal. When he is hungry, he will eat...even if his favorite food is nowhere to be found. Thus, food jags last as long as adults cater to them.

A food jag is different from food refusal, although it might be accompanied by it. One can refuse food without having a particular food jag. For example, a toddler hates the taste of green beans and refuses to eat them. He will, however, eat other foods. In this case, a toddler refuses only one food.

Some toddlers refuse many foods, especially if mealtime becomes a battle between parent and child. In this scenario, a child initially wants to play with food; the parent wants her to eat. The child throws the food on the floor; the parent responds by giving more food or trying to force the child to eat. The child might revert to a temper tantrum, or she might just keep throwing food around. The parent is not amused but becomes concerned that the child needs something to eat. So the parent offers the child something she knows she will eat—a cookie, candy, french fries. Voilà! The child has gotten what she wants, and she is likely to try this the next time she eats.

Like food jags, food refusal lasts as long as adults cater to them.

### Battles over toileting

*So proud of his stool—*
*blood-curdling screaming when flushed.*
*"Me want it," he sobs.*

Most toddlers are not ready to be toilet trained until well past their second birthday, for anatomic and physiologic reasons. A child cannot be toilet trained until he makes a connection between the sensation in his bladder or rectum and using the toilet. Until that connection can be made, getting the child to the toilet on time will be "hit or miss."

That does not stop some parents from trying to make it happen before that second birthday. Most parents are not trying to be mean about training. They *think* their child is ready by the cues he occasionally gives when he needs to use the toilet. Or, they want their child to wear "grownup" underwear. Or, they're tired of diapers.

Toilet battles occur as a child tries to maintain his autonomy, and they are more marked with stooling than with urination. After all, a child produces an object—a stool. He is fascinated by it, and it is his. He does not share the adult horror at touching it or wanting to save it. He seems not to be disturbed by its odor.

When a parent wants to flush the stool away, the toddler might object loudly: it's as if he's saying, "That's mine, and I want it!" This is one type of toilet battle.

Another type is a child's refusal to use the toilet, preferring to stool in his underwear. This usually occurs when a parent has placed the child in underwear prematurely. Perhaps, the child simply doesn't care about the underwear, or perhaps he is afraid of the toilet. Most likely, it is neither of these reasons. He might just not be aware of the full rectum and the need to get to the toilet. So, an accident happens. If the parent is calm about it, no harm is done. It is only when the parent overreacts (and, remember, we are talking about children too young for toilet training) that a battle can occur, as the parent *insists* that the child can stool in the toilet "if he wanted to." The child, for one reason or another, can't, so the child does what he can do, which is not what the parent wants.

A third type of battle is a child who refuses to have a bowel movement because it is painful to do so. Such a child will try to hold onto his stool for as long as he can. Impaction can result, with liquid stool overflowing, making the parent think that the child is indeed stooling. Painful bowel movements can be related to constipation with large, hard stools, or tears in the anal tissue that are irritated or torn as the anus stretches to accommodate the large stool.

Toilet battles are minimized by waiting until a child is old enough to understand what a toilet is for and what a parent wants him to do there. He should be able to connect the sensation of a full bladder or rectum with urinating or stooling. A parent should respect the child's affection for his stool without going overboard. A child who seems afraid of the toilet might first need to become comfortable with a potty chair. Finally, if a child seems as if he is in pain when passing a stool, he should be seen by his doctor.

## Summary • Questions • Resources

In toddlerhood, the young child is clearly no longer a baby as she becomes more and more independent, amasses a vocabulary, understands even more words than she can say, imitates (quite well) everything she sees, engages in simple rituals, and begins to have an understanding of right and wrong. She can be a joy, and she can be quite maddening when some of her less attractive phases kick in! She is the unique person that God created her to be, and adults should be humbled by that, guiding her to be the best that she can be in light of her gifts and limitations.

## *Questions—Catechists*

- What advice would you give a parent whose eighteen-month-old is banging a noisy toy on the pew in church?

- What advice would you give a parent whose two-year-old is having a full-blown temper tantrum?

- What would you say to a parent who is making fun of a two-and-one-half-year-old who is frightened of something or who needs her transitional object (that is, security blanket)?

## *Questions—Parents*

- At what age do you think a child should be toilet trained and why?

- Are there any fears that you believe are "silly" for a child to have? What are they? What fears do you remember having as a child?

- In your mind, what makes a toddler "too active"? In other words, what separates a normally active toddler from a child who is "hyperactive"?

### Resources

Erikson, Erik: *Childhood and Society.* New York: WW Norton & Co., 1985 [especially chapter 7].

Fowler, James: *Stages of Faith: The Psychology of Human Development and the Quest for Meaning.* San Francisco: HarperSanFrancisco, 1995 [especially chapter 15].

Kuhmerker, Lisa: *The Kohlberg Legacy for the Helping Professions.* Birmingham, Ala.: R.E.P. Books, 1991 [especially table on pages 28–29].

McMillan, Julia and Catherine DeAngelis, Ralph Feigin, and Joseph Worshaw (eds): *Oski's Pediatrics: Principles and Practices, Third Edition.* Philadelphia: Lippincott Williams & Wilkins, 1999 [especially tables 119–1; 119–2; 120–1; 120–2; 395–1].

Shelov, Steven (ed): *(The American Academy of Pediatrics) Caring for Your Baby and Young Child, Birth to Age 5.* New York: Bantam Books, 1991. [Excellent reference book.]

Siberry, George, and Robert Iannone (eds): *The Harriet Lane Handbook.* St. Louis: Mosby, 2000 [especially chapter 9].

Singer, Dorothy, and Tracey Revenson: *A Piaget Primer: How a Child Thinks.* New York: New American Library, 1978 [especially chapter 2].

# PRESCHOOL YEARS

· · · · · ·

*Gazing intently*
*at three dancing flames on cake—*
*sad to blow them out.*

· · ·

*Teetering in shoes*
*made for big girls, not for her.*
*So pretty! She laughs.*

The preschool years are generally the first time that religious educators have children for a set period each week. Children might or might not have received any religious education from their parents, so it is to be expected that for some children this will be a completely novel experience. In addition, some children might not have been away from their parents, making their adjustment to a class situation difficult.

## Physical Development—Gross Motor

*Dreaming of swinging*
*so high (even on her porch)*
*that she kisses clouds.*

*Chasing his shadow—*
*wondering why it always*
*eludes swift capture.*

Preschoolers love to move! They run, jump, hop, kick balls, and sway to music. Many cannot sit still for all but the briefest of periods. This does not mean they are hyperactive—they are simply *normal*. They have so much energy. And so, it is good to make use of that energy by permitting children to learn by doing. This "learning" includes not only classroom lessons but also the lessons about daily life and day-to-day activities.

It is at this age that little boys will act like little boys, as they have "battles" so they can pretend to be soldiers; "fires" so they can pretend to be firemen; "tools" so they can pretend to be repairmen. Little girls will pretend to go to the mall to shop; fix meals in the kitchen; take care of their "children" (for instance dolls and so forth). All of these activities are very physical, requiring large muscles to move, lift, hammer, saw, carry, and so on.

The activities that children imitate are those that they see most commonly. They love to imitate those who are important to them, so such significant adults (parents, teachers, and so forth) need to ensure that they are the best role models that they can be in terms of their behaviors in front of children. For example, a preschooler is as likely to imitate an obscene gesture as she is a gesture of blessing, for she doesn't know the difference. If she experiences more obscene gestures than ones of blessing, her imitative play will contain a surplus of such undesirable gestures.

## Physical Development—Fine Motor

*Knows well how to print
her whole name but only when
sticking her tongue out.*

• • •

*Bubbles in the bath—
child entranced by each one, but
pops them, ne'ertheless.*

Preschoolers' hand-eye coordination is improving all the time. Thus, they are more likely to throw a ball accurately and use building blocks to actually make a structure. Their ability to color within the lines is improving, and that is wonderful because they love to color! Children of this age like to imitate what others draw. A child can copy a circle by three years, a cross by three and a half years, a square by four years, and a triangle by five years; these imitations will not look exactly like the "real" figures, but so what? This is the way that children learn—through practice. Preschoolers also love to draw spontaneously, and that should be encouraged. Their drawings will not look like those of older children, and, sometimes, the identity of what they have drawn needs clarification. For example, a three-year-old can draw a "person," but the figure usually has only a head and one other body part. Preschoolers also tend to use unusual colors for common things, for example, drawing a red sun. These drawings should not be ridiculed, but should, instead, elicit the reasons for choosing the color(s) they did.

To use eating utensils, a child's fine-motor skills must be

developed. Preschoolers can generally eat neatly (when they want to), and using utensils such as a fork or spoon is not a problem. Like many adults, they still prefer to use their fingers for certain foods.

In terms of using the bathroom, they usually can do so without difficulty, unless they are wearing "complicated" clothes with lots of fasteners or they are having a problem like diarrhea, which might interfere with their making it to the toilet in time. Although they are capable of washing their hands well, they often don't, as they go through the motions— with cold water! Because proper hand-washing is so important to curtail the spread of germs, supervision is needed for hand-washing to ensure it is done properly with this age group.

## Physical Development— Sleep, Diet, and Elimination

Most preschoolers sleep through the night (eight to ten hours) and might also still take a one- or two-hour nap during the day.

Generally, preschoolers have good appetites, although they might "hate" vegetables and refuse to eat them. They usually have preferred foods, but, unfortunately, these are often the foods with the highest content of sugar, salt, or fat. Why? Because they taste good! Preschoolers are particularly fond of fast foods. Parents should limit their preschoolers' intake of such foods, which should *not* usually be used as rewards or punishments for behavior. After all, food is for nourishment, not for discipline.

Most preschoolers urinate four to six times per day and have a bowel movement every day or every other day.

## Psychological/Emotional Development

*So many presents—*
*but which one to open first?*
*Frustrated, she cries.*

• • •

*Atop old brick wall*
*boy-child is king, surveying*
*his subjects below.*

Most preschoolers are happy, bubbly people who love to talk and interact with others. Many of them like to talk *a lot*, and they will even talk to themselves when no one else is around! Unless a child seems particularly anxious, needing to fill every moment with talk, one can probably assume that a child's chattiness is normal. A preschooler's growth in vocabulary is truly phenomenal. Most three-year-olds have about a 500 to 1,000-word vocabulary and can routinely compose simple three-word sentences. By the time that they are five years old, they have about a 2,000-word vocabulary and can compose more complicated sentences.

Preschoolers love to tell stories, and sometimes, their ability to tell reality from fiction is limited. This makes it hard to determine whether a child is willfully lying or merely confusing reality with her own wishes. Most of the time they are not lying, but because they want things to be a certain way, they believe that they really *are* that way. For example, because they really *want* to be good, they might lie when they are asked if they did something wrong that they obviously did. If one confronts such a child, she might persist in her lie because she is afraid that she will be punished. Adults do well to understand such behavior sympathetically, saying something like, "I know you want to be good and not drop the glass. So, let's think of ways that you won't drop the glass next time." By this response, the adult sends the message that he knows the child did the act, but is willing to explore ways that it might not happen the next time. In this way, no arguments are necessary.

Preschoolers can be very loud, as they have not learned what an appropriate volume for ordinary speech is. They are also learning to handle their frustrations more with words than with tantrums. Although they will have many lapses, this is a stage of real maturation for them, so adults need to be tolerant when the lapses occur.

Temperamentally, like adults, some children are overtly affectionate while others are not. Like many adults, some are shy and not very talkative. Although extreme shyness or virtual paralysis in a group is always worrisome, some children appear shyer than they actually are. For example, if a slightly shy child is around a group of rowdy children, she will appear shyer than she really is. With children more like her, she might actually be one of the noisier ones! Shy children should be gently encouraged to speak and take part in group activities.

Erik Erikson noted that the developmental task to be achieved by preschoolers is *initiative vs. guilt.* With their growing autonomy, preschoolers begin to take initiative in getting things done. Sometimes, because they really are still inexperienced, their attempts result in more work for others. That might cause them guilt, especially if their unsuccessful attempts are handled badly. If this happens often enough, preschoolers might become afraid to try anything new or on their own. That is why it is so important for parents and teachers to handle mistakes gently and encouragingly. When a child knows that she is loved for herself, regardless of the mistakes she makes, she has a better chance of becoming a well-adjusted older child and teen than she would if she believes that she is only loved for what she can do.

## Cognitive Development

*Five-year-old wonders*
*how to keep melting ice cream*
*in its soggy cone.*

• • •

*Cannot believe that*
*moon is not talking to her—*
*she calls it moonspeak.*

Jean Piaget noted that preschoolers are in a *preoperational* stage of cognitive development. Preoperational means that the associations that these young children make are not logical in the way we adults understand logic. The associations make perfect sense to them, but not to older children or adults who are more accustomed to logical reasoning. Preschoolers make sense of their world through fantasies and unusual insights. This is normal and should not be discouraged, even though it seems not to be the "right" way of thinking about things or solving a problem.

Because of their own "logic," there are some things that

preschoolers cannot do very well, and adults make a mistake if they expect them to do so. They cannot understand that the same amount of milk poured first into a small glass and then into a larger one still remains the same amount. They will invariably note that the large glass has more...even when they are shown to be the same! They are not good at categorizing things, so if asked for his favorite vegetables, a preschooler might say, "Hot dogs!" Similarly, young children do not remember the sequence of stories well. They might be able to note the highlights of a story, but they cannot place them in proper order. Finally, children expect that if one thing causes another, then the other causes the first. So, if the rain soaks a tablecloth on the picnic table, when the tablecloth is again wet (for whatever reason), a preschooler is likely to believe that it is going to rain. In other words, she doesn't understand that associations are not causations.

Even in the midst of all this, preschoolers love to learn, and they seem to accumulate facts like corners accumulate dust balls! The most common question children of this age ask is "Why?" and they can ask it repeatedly. They are not trying to be annoying; they simply want to understand what is happening and then try to make associations with other things that they already know. Preschoolers love to put large puzzles together. This is important on two developmental counts: first, their fine-motor skills allow them to manipulate the puzzle parts into place; second, their ability to recognize different shapes helps them find the right place for each puzzle part.

If they have been exposed to books at home, most preschoolers enjoy books enormously. Many preschoolers know the alphabet and how to spell their name. These children might also know how to read a little. This should be encouraged but not expected. Not every preschooler knows the alphabet or can read, and some of their inability might be because they were not given sufficient stimulation at home. Some children pretend to read, pointing at words and saying either the story or something else. Although, objectively, what they're doing is wrong (the printed words might not match what the child is saying), the child's action demonstrates that she knows that printed words mean something. And *that* is a large achievement because, after all, words do not look like the thing they represent!

Preschoolers can know thousands of words, including some words we would prefer them not to know. Like sponges pick up water, preschoolers pick up words from those around them. If encouraged to learn colors, children of this age master colors easily. The best way for children of this age to learn anything is to make a game of it, because they love games. They also love jokes and rhymes, even though the jokes might seem "dumb" to adults and the rhymes seem lame. In fact, many children learn numbers, letters, and new words through rhyming games.

"Pretend" games or fantasies should never be discounted as a way of learning. In fact, it is through their imaginations that many children can practice different ways of handling situations. In the preschool years, these situations can be quite imaginative (for example, a princess being rescued from a pirate), but these can help them handle their fears and give them some power. As they become older, the situations of their fantasies become more lifelike.

## Social Development

*Sister hits brother.*
*Wailing! Both appeal to mom—*
*risky to take sides.*

• • •

*Four-year-old eager*
*to help daddy with "men" chores;*
*older brother smirks.*

Preschoolers are learning to get along with large groups of children, some of whom they might not like or who are not like them in obvious ways. This might be the first time that they have had to be with so many other children. Although preschoolers do not usually have "best" friends in the sense that older children and adults understand friendship, they do have friends with whom they prefer to sit or play. That is normal. Yet, preschoolers are very open to the idea that every person might be a friend, and one of the ways they are dissuaded from this point of view is if they receive bad treatment by a child or if an adult comments that certain children (or adults) aren't "nice."

Playing for young children gradually progresses from "parallel" play to interactive play over the preschool years. Parallel play means that although children are seated side by side, they are not actually playing *with* each other. In other words, each child is doing his own thing. Interactive play, on the other hand, means that the children are playing together, whether harmoniously or not! Problems with interactive play, at this age, are frequently related to whose turn it is. This is related to sharing.

Preschoolers do need to learn to share, and that might be a major task for those who have no siblings and for those who have an endless supply of toys. It is common to see several children "fighting" over a single toy in a room filled with other toys, because children live in the moment. What they want, they want now. If others want a particular toy, then it becomes even more attractive! Preschoolers are not highly skilled at putting themselves in another's place. That's a hard concept for them to grasp, because they see everything from their own perspective. Even their games start with each child's concept of the rules, not the actual rules themselves. So, when a child wants his turn, he is thinking by his rules, that is, it's his turn, regardless of the facts! Empathy is just beginning in the preschool years, and it will take several years to get it right. As we all know, some individuals have lifelong problems with placing themselves in another's place.

## Moral Development

*Plotting her revenge*
*poor pink pillow takes beating*
*from such little fists.*

• • •

*Chocolate candy*
*always the best reward when*
*he's been good all day.*

Preschoolers are very interested in avoiding punishment. Because they understand that those older than them have superior power, they will do what is right or expected of them to avoid any consequences of misbehavior. This is Kohlberg's first stage of moral development, *doing what is right to avoid punishment*, and it can be quite effective in shaping behavior. Unfortunately, some children are overly controlled by physical punishment and can be afraid to move an inch. Such "obedience" is based more on fear of being hurt than on trying to do the right thing. Other children of this age will do the right thing or what is expected of them only to please significant persons in their lives. Although the motive is laudable, they still are several years away from doing the right thing *because* it is the right thing.

Preschoolers do not understand the idea of motivation or intention, so they believe that if someone breaks two toys accidentally (for example, by helping his mother clean up), he did worse than someone breaking one toy because he threw it on purpose. For older children and adults, motivation is very important; for preschoolers, it's meaningless. For them, two is greater than one, so the first child must be "badder" and should receive harsher punishment than the second child, especially if the child comes from a home where mistakes are handled harshly. Although preschoolers certainly need limits, those limits need to be clear and sympathetically crafted by the adults caring for them.

## Spiritual Development

*Gazing at the sky*
*knowing she sees Jesus, but*
*no one believes her.*

• • •

*Jesus on a cross*
*so scary her small frame shakes;*
*why'd he have to die?*

James Fowler called the stage of preschooler faith development *intuitive-projective*. An intuition is having a sense about something, even though one has not been taught about it, heard about it, or seen it. Young children have an intuition about God. Their ideas are not the same as that of older children and adults, and might even seem rather strange. Yet, the truth of what young children are saying is not necessarily wrong. For example, when asked what does she think of when she hears the word *God*, a four-year-old might say, "Chocolate ice cream!" Why? Because that's her favorite food in the whole world and God is her favorite person! Fowler's stage is very much related to Jean Piaget's *preoperational* stage.

Young children can also project. Projection is placing onto a new person, situation, place, or thing one's experiences with similar persons, situations, places, or things from the past. Projections can be neutral, such as calling a fox a dog because it walks on four legs, has a tail, pointed ears, and has a face like a dog. They can also be positive or negative, such as attributing to a stranger the admired or despised characteristics (real or imagined) of other persons from that stranger's ethnic group. Young children can imagine that God is exactly like their mother or father, projecting onto God the positive (or negative) attributes of the parent. So, a three-year-old can say that "If you're not good, God will squish you like a bug," because that's what he's seen his father do with unwanted insects. Alternatively, a three-year-old can say, "God loves me a lot, just like a daddy does," because that is his experience.

## Major Phases Beginning in Preschool Years

### Fears

*Every night the same*
*in and out of her dark room—*
*wants mom's room instead.*

All human beings have fears. In the preschool years, fears might be of things that are not real. Because children of this age have such vivid imaginations and they have difficulty separating reality from fantasy, they might be afraid of dragons, pirates, and other characters that they've heard about in books or seen on electronic media. These fears are best met by helping the child "do" things that make the feared objects or persons go away; these things might be quite fanciful themselves! Adult ridicule of the fears does not help (such as saying: "You're afraid of dragons? I thought you were a big boy!"). Instead it often shames the child.

Other children have fears that are based in reality. A child who has been bitten by a dog or has heard gunshots has legitimate reasons for fear. Furthermore, since these fears are based in reality, much time might be needed to move beyond the fears (if, indeed, that ever happens). As noted in the previous paragraph, adult ridicule does not help, and, in these situations, it might hurt. After all, has the adult been bitten by a dog? Does she understand how terrifying that is? When an adult trivializes a child's fears, she can feel alone when she most needs help.

*"Gimme!" or "I want it."*
*Obnoxious whining*
*never ending—'cuz it works!*
*Gets her way each time.*

As noted earlier, children of this age see things only from their perspective. So, when they want something (a toy, a turn, individual attention), they want it now! Furthermore, because they are just beginning to really understand time, they have great difficulty in delaying gratification. Many preschoolers simply do not understand what "five minutes" means or how that is different from ten minutes or even an hour. (As an aside, this is why children repeatedly ask, "Are we there yet?" when riding in a car, driven by a parent who says, "We'll be there in an hour.") This is a normal developmental stage and does not mean that the child is destined to be selfish forever.

Many children whine to get what they want. Because most adults *hate* the sound of whining, they will give in to the whining child just to make the noise stop. Naturally, the child understands that, using whining quite effectively. The way to encourage a child to stop whining is to say something like, "I really can't understand you when you talk like that. If you talk normally (or like you usually do), then I might be able to understand you better so we could talk." Giving in to whining only perpetuates it.

In addition, many children have the "gimmes." They see so much in stores, on television, at their friends' houses, that they want it all. Because they can only think of things from their own perspective, they demand those things that they want. After all, if a friend has a toy, why can't he? If there are so many toys in the store, why can't he have some of them? If a toy is shown (a lot) on television, it must mean that everyone has it except him. In this last example, because a preschooler cannot always separate reality from fantasy, he *really* believes that *only* he lacks the toy. Parents and other significant adults must set age-appropriate limits on the number of toys or turns any one child has. As was mentioned earlier, it is *hard* to learn to share.

### *Sibling rivalry*

*Angrily crying—*
*brother pulled her hair (again).*
*She plots sweet revenge.*

It is true that toddlers can be jealous of a new sibling, and, because they are so immature, they react in ways that treat the infant like a toy or an object. They really do not understand their strength or the fact that they were once that small. They don't even understand that the infant is a person like them. So, although their actions cannot be permitted, they make sense…from a toddler's point of view.

In the preschool years, children understand that the new baby is not a toy and is, in fact, a new person. Yet, they too, need to be reminded to be gentle with their new sibling. In the name of "helping" a parent, a preschooler might imitate (either poorly or accurately) how she has seen her parents treat the baby. For example, if the parents "pat" the baby's back to comfort him when he's crying, his three-year-old sister might imitate that by hitting him hard when he cries. If a parent pours a little powder on his bottom during diaper changes, his sister might pour the entire container.

Although those might be excused in the name of trying to help, some preschoolers really don't like an infant sibling in terms of the attention he garners from the parents. They might intentionally try to hurt a younger sibling, such as squeezing too hard or hitting. Or they may regress back to the time when they received more attention from their parents. The toilet-trained four-year-old might start wetting her pants so that her parents will help her with toileting again. The three-year-old might start waking up at night to get his parents to come to *his* room. The five-year-old might start sucking his thumb again to comfort himself, something he hasn't done since he was two years old. All of these indicate that the child is stressed by the new sibling and that parents and other significant adults need to give the child some additional attention. This can be extremely difficult for parents who might themselves be exhausted and feel like they have no additional time. Other significant adults can make a difference in this regard.

*Transitional objects*
(AKA *"security blankets"*)
*Such a big boy 'cept
for one little thing; blankie!
Needs it to survive.*

Transitional objects were discussed in the section "Toddler-hood." Their use can last into the early preschool years, especially if a child has never been away from his parents before. Because it is a way of dealing with stress, the use of transitional objects usually decreases as a child feels more comfortable in her surroundings. It also decreases when a child sees that his peers do not carry a "blankie" around with them.

So, patience is in order. If a child needs her security object for a prolonged period of time, or if she becomes hysterical if she is separated—even briefly—from it, a conference with her parents is in order.

## Summary • Questions • Resources

Is there anyone more delightful than a healthy, happy pre-schooler? Unless he is given the message that he is "no good," he will be in love with life and everything that he sees, al-though sometimes fears (occasionally irrational) might sur-face. Eager to engage every created thing, he is in constant motion, usually talking or singing, constantly asking "Why?" not because he wants to irritate but mostly because he wants to know. Yet, he can act according to his own whims and desires, being selfish, demanding, and aggressive, but might curtail such behavior if there is a consistent penalty for acting badly. God is very real to him, as he chats with or sings to God or imitates what happens at church in his play. Adults do well to watch in awe.

## Questions—Catechists

- How would you manage a situation in which a five-year-old child continues to talk out of turn in class or talks so much that no one else has a turn to speak? When would you bring the situation to the attention of the child's parent, and how would you do so?

- How would you manage a situation in which 2 four-year-old children are squabbling over the same toy?

- What would you say to a five-year-old who wants everything that he sees? What would you do if he tries to destroy anything that he can't have?

## Questions—Parents

- What is your reaction when your preschooler says a "bad" word? What might you say to dissuade him from saying it again?

- What is an appropriate response to a four-year-old who is too rough with her new baby brother?

- What are appropriate and inappropriate ways of disciplining a five-year-old who "tells stories"?

## Resources

Erikson, Erik: *Childhood and Society.* New York: WW Norton & Co., 1985 [especially chapter 7].

Fowler, James: *Stages of Faith: The Psychology of Human Development and the Quest for Meaning.* San Francisco: HarperSanFrancisco, 1995 [especially chapter 16].

Kuhmerker, Lisa: *The Kohlberg Legacy for the Helping Professions.* Birmingham, Ala.: R.E.P. Books, 1991 [especially table on pages 28–29].

McMillan, Julia, Catherine DeAngelis, Ralph Feigin, and Joseph Worshaw (eds): *Oski's Pediatrics: Principles and Practices, Third Edition.* Philadelphia: Lippincott Williams & Wilkins, 1999 [especially tables 119–1; 119–2; 120–1; 120–2; 395–1].

Shelov, Steven (ed): *(The American Academy of Pediatrics) Caring for Your Baby and Young Child, Birth to Age 5.* New York: Bantam Books, 1991. [Excellent reference book.]

Siberry, George, and Robert Iannone (eds): *The Harriet Lane Handbook.* St. Louis: Mosby, 2000 [especially chapter 9].

Singer, Dorothy, and Tracey Revenson: *A Piaget Primer: How a Child Thinks.* New York: New American Library, 1978 [especially chapter 2].

# EARLY ELEMENTARY SCHOOL YEARS

· · · · · ·

*Stomping in puddles*
*as big as the moon, he laughs*
*all the way back home.*

· · ·

*Awning of red hair*
*shades freckles a-plenty 'round*
*bespectacled eyes.*

Once in elementary school, children realize that they are no longer "little kids" but are entering the adult world of learning and work. They might be meeting other children who are not very much like them for the first time. Also, perhaps for the first time, a child might feel the need to compete, especially if he has a teacher who encourages competition or "ranks" children according to abilities. He might get a sense of his own skills and inadequacies. First grade might be the first time that religious educators have some children for a set period each week. Children might or might not have received any religious education from their parents, so it is to be expected that for some children this will be a completely new experience. In addition, a few children might not have been away from their parents, making their adjustment to a class situation difficult.

## Physical Development—Gross Motor

*Over and over*
*he falls! wondering how one*
*stays upright on ice.*

• • •

*Shiny bicycle*
*waiting for first ride. Pity!*
*Training wheels needed.*

Physical abilities continue to improve as a child matures. Children can now run faster, throw and kick harder, carry heavier loads, jump from higher levels, jump rope more accurately. In all of these activities, they generally show more endurance. This is because of the increasing growth and development of their muscles and nervous systems. Some parents discover that their children have a special kinesthetic sense and help them develop that by providing dancing lessons, gymnastic classes, participation in team sports, and so forth. All of this should be done in the sense of fun and enjoyment, since it is all too easy for children to fall into a competitive mode at this age, especially if significant adults in their lives are pushing them to compete or if these adults feel that any failures are embarrassing.

## Physical Development—Fine Motor

*Awkwardly holding*
*knitting needles, so mammoth*
*for her little hands.*

• • •

*Little hands finger*
*piano keys. Sounds erupt!*
*Child can't help laughing.*

Children of this age generally have ever-improving hand-eye coordination. Their ability to draw more complicated shapes—either by copying them or doing so spontaneously—improves with age, especially if they are encouraged to draw. Although at the beginning of this age, printing and handwriting might be sloppy, by the preteens years, most children can print and write neatly if they take their time. Similarly, most children of this age can color neatly or accurately cut out an object from paper if they take their time. As was true for gross-motor skills, some children will have a special ability in this department, as they can—seemingly effortlessly—draw, paint, make objects that other children their age cannot. Naturally, such skills improve with time and practice, which is why encouragement is so important.

Children of this age usually can use eating utensils well and can certainly dress themselves, although parents might not like either what they choose to eat or wear! In fact, although they know their colors well, they might mix unusual colors because they don't care or because other children are wearing the same color combinations. Peer influence is important even at this age (see below).

Almost the only dressing problem that children have at this age is tying their shoes. For some children, it takes much practice to figure out and master those loops!

## Physical Development—
## Sleep, Diet, and Elimination

Children of this age usually need eight to ten hours of sleep each night. Naps are usually not taken. This means that if a child stays up late, she *will* be tired the next day.

Young elementary schoolchildren usually have very good appetites, although they still might not be too fond of vegetables! Like other ages, they too like fast foods and foods that are sugary, salty, or fatty, because such foods usually taste good. Such foods should be limited in the diets of young elementary school-age children. Although it is uncommon, some girls of this age might become weight conscious, especially if they have been teased about being "pudgy" by family members or friends. This might signal a red flag for future problems with weight. See the discussion in the preteen chapter.

By this age, most children have established a normal elimination pattern. This usually means one bowel movement every day or every other day, and three to six urinations each day; the latter obviously varies by the volume of liquid ingested.

## Psychological/Emotional Development

*Bored since second grade,*
*now the class funster, giving*
*him something to do.*

• • •

*No one else at home...*
*but him. Opportunities!*
*Just where to begin?*

Children of this age are generally happy and excited about life. They have a real eagerness to obtain as many experiences as they can and to enjoy them. They need unconditional love from their parents to best enjoy their experiences without fearing that if they make mistakes (as they will), they won't be loved. Although they are still very much like preschoolers in some ways, their increasing maturity means that they might begin to think before they blurt something out, to ponder before they act. They are increasingly interested in what others think of them and will try to do things to please others, especially their parents and teachers. Particularly shy or tentative children might be even more responsive to what the adults in their lives want than will other children. As with preschoolers, shy, tentative children might need more encouragement than do more outgoing children.

Erik Erikson's stage for this age group is called *industry vs. inferiority*. Children are often told, "Work hard, and you'll do better." Once in school, many children do work hard, yet they do not reap the rewards of that hard work.

No matter how hard a boy studies, he never gets an A. No matter how many times a girl practices the piano, she always makes many mistakes. Such "failures" might demoralize such children, especially if they are compared to others whose achievements seem to come effortlessly. That is why it is so important for parents and teachers to help a child discover an area (or areas) in which she has competence, or better yet, an area at which she can really excel. Finding even one such area helps to build a child's self-esteem, for if a child can see herself as competent in one area, she can muster the courage to explore other areas; if she believes that she can succeed in one area, she can believe that she can succeed in another.

## Cognitive Development

*Chewing on pencil,*
*hot tears smudging her efforts—*
*homework never ends.*

• • •

*Fails to understand*
*the point of composition—*
*rather talk than write.*

Jean Piaget noted that children of this age learn through *concrete operations*. In other words, they need concrete objects to learn skills. For example, to learn addition and subtraction, initially a teacher might line up eight candies, subtract two, and ask how many are left. When the children count six, the teacher can note that eight minus two is always six. Then, the teacher can add the two candies to the other six. He again asks the class how many candies there are. When the children count eight, he can note that six plus two is always eight. Concrete objects can be used for learning many subjects, such as spelling, arithmetic, geography, and science. Because there is usually only one right answer for spelling words or math problems, children of this age are very literal: it's either right or wrong.

Because children of this age are entering formal education (perhaps for the first time), they are constantly learning new things, such as letters, words, numbers, arithmetic actions, and spelling. For children with some confidence in their ability to successfully learn new information, this is a wonderful experience. For children who doubt their abilities, it can be overwhelming, disheartening, and even frightening. When children have parents who were, themselves, unsuccessful students or have parents who discount their abilities to succeed, children can become even more fearful or disheartened. If children require medication in order for them to better attend to learning, they might even feel that their brains are abnormal, especially if they are teased by classmates, friends, or siblings. *Anything* that interferes with a child's ability to learn must be discovered and dealt with promptly if the child is to experience school and, indeed, all learning as a positive.

Children of this age are making associations among the many things they are learning to create a seamless whole in terms of their knowledge. Such integration should be greatly encouraged. In addition to speaking their ideas, they are learning to communicate in a written form, creating sentences and paragraphs of ideas. This is usually a very liberating experience, although for children who do not write well, it might be just the opposite. Such children might be better able to express themselves through poetry, art, or music, and that should be encouraged. Communication—through speech, written forms, or art—is important at this age because it helps to teach a child that there might be many ways to express the same concept, a wonderful lesson for them to learn in the classroom and in life. When one way of expression doesn't work well, there are usually other ways to make the point.

At this age, children love jokes, riddles, and humor, and their ability in this area increases as they become older. For example, a young elementary schoolchild will not understand a pun. But the elementary schoolchild who is bordering on the preteen years not only is likely to "get it," but is also likely to craft one of her own. Such an inventive use of language is a very positive aspect of cognitive development. And, in terms of humor in general, childhood *should* be fun. Children should laugh often. The beneficial psychological effects of a good laugh have been known for some time. Now, investigators have even noted that there are *physical* effects of a good laugh, as laughing seems to open up some blood vessels, improving blood flow. How good it is for children to get in the habit of hearty laughter each day, and how good it would be for them (and for adults) if they could see such modeling from the significant adults in their lives!

Games of "let's pretend" and fantasies are important at this age and would only be a source of concern if a child preferred personal fantasy to any interaction with other children or adults. Through fantasies, children might be able to imagine themselves winning the spelling bee or hitting the home run. Such fantasies help the speller remember the words with which she has trouble or helps the batter think about his swing. For children who are readers, many of their fantasies emerge from what they have read, and that is wonderful. Children might also be able to "re-play" a real-life situation that happened with others, exploring ways that it could have been handled differently, or thinking through the various consequences of any actions they might take.

## Social Development

*Sneaking a look at*
*his sister and her boyfriend*
*kissing—he feels sick.*

• • •

*Eating lunch alone—*
*best friend prefers another—*
*tears fall on sandwich.*

Children of this age are comfortable being around adults. They also enjoy being in same-sex peer groups, and they especially like group activities such as games or socializing with one another. Parties are very popular at this age. Although parties are a hit in the preschool years, because children of that age are much more self-centered, such parties are more likely to disintegrate into tears, as one child wants something that another has. The increased maturity of the early elementary schoolchild means that everyone can have a good time.

Perhaps the greatest social step at this age is the development of close friendships with only one or two other children. Although, at this age, one's "best" friend might change from one week to the next because of little squabbles, the milestone of "best" friend is an important one. When one becomes another's "best" friend, one must learn that one cannot always have his way; the friend gets his way sometimes. So, give and take or *reciprocity* is the first lesson. If one considers another his best friend, he will be there for him, even if other children are teasing him about it. *Loyalty* is another important lesson. If one is another's best friend, he will keep his promises to that friend, even if it's inconvenient to do so. *Generosity* is yet another lesson. Having a best friend helps children move beyond self-focus toward an other-focus. All of this encourages the growth of empathy.

In terms of public behavior, children of this age know how to behave in a public space and are usually eager to do so. Unlike their younger counterparts who might have a "meltdown" when things don't go their way, elementary schoolchildren are interested enough in what others will think of them to watch their public behavior in most situations. In fact, what others will think, unfortunately, drives many children's behavior, especially those who are insecure about their abilities. They will want to "fit in" with a group whom they admire. Because some children can be cruel, they might ridicule any differences they detect in another child, leading to unhappiness in the child so targeted.

## Moral Development

*Self-appointed snitch—*
*considers herself teacher's*
*trustworthy ally.*

• • •

*Hamster in toilet*
*("was an accident, I swear!")*
*Lesson? R.I.P.*

As they enter school, many children are still in Lawrence Kohlberg's first stage of moral development of doing the right thing to avoid punishment. Naturally, some children remain in that stage for a long period of time, usually because of parental disciplinary practices. For most children, as they mature, they usually move to Kohlberg's second stage, *doing the right thing to satisfy their own needs or to appear good in others' estimation.* Children of this age are still relatively self-centered, so it is natural that they seek to satisfy their own wants. Because children of this age are also interested in what others think, especially those in authority or power, they want to be held in high esteem by such persons. That is why they will "announce" that they did the right thing. They want the adult to, at least, know it and, ideally, praise them, especially if they need that kind of recognition from an authority figure. That is also one reason why some children become "snitches" or "tattlers": they want the parent, teacher, or other adult to know that *they* are on the side of authority and that other individuals are not.

At this age, children appeal to rules that are external to

themselves. They expect others to follow the rules exactly as they have been written (or said) especially if the rule was given by an authority figure or someone they trust. Furthermore, they expect predictable consequences if rules are not obeyed. In fact, children of this age can be harsher in their discipline than are adults. They need a standard to guide their behavior, and because the rule is "outside" them, it's assumed to be fair. And, fairness is a big issue at this age, but fairness means that all are treated equally, not that all are treated according to their skills, or lack thereof. Such understanding will take several more years to develop. That explains why children of this age might cry, "Not fair!" when a teacher permits a child with vision problems to have a few extra minutes to finish an assignment. The children believe that fairness means that the teacher should treat everyone equally, no matter what. As an adult, the teacher understands fairness as meaning that each child have an approximately equal chance of succeeding in a task. So, for her, making allowances "levels the playing field," and is fair.

Children need good role models acting in a morally responsible fashion so that they can learn more about right and wrong and how one's actions affect others. This is so important that it cannot be overstated. When children see significant adults "bending the rules," they become confused and wonder exactly what the right course of action really is. On the other hand, even though they need rules and limits, they also need to be exposed to why (and when) exceptions can be made to certain rules or limits. Because at their age they don't believe in exceptions, they also need to know how a legitimate exception differs from "bending the rules."

There is nothing wrong with a young child doing the right thing to appear good in another's eyes, because, in the end, the right thing was done. If she remains in that stage, however, she will never learn how to judge an action on its own merits and might be subject to the fickleness of human opinion, hardly a firm foundation for the moral life. The goal is to do the right thing even when no one else is around; that is the beginning of the internal moral compass. The ability to do the right thing even when one is alone is just beginning at this age and will take years to become entrenched.

## Spiritual Development

*Blessing himself with*
*holy water so pristine,*
*surely he's transformed.*

• • •

*Prayers not answered—*
*hot tears streaming down her face*
*angry at her God.*

James Fowler's stage for this age group is called *mythic-literal*. Children of this age love myths, those stories where virtues are highlighted, where good wins out over bad. The bigger the story, the better; the stronger the hero (or heroine), the better. So, at this age, children love Scripture stories in which mighty deeds are done, whether it's Moses parting the Red Sea or Jesus feeding the multitudes with very little food. Such stories spark children's imaginations, and they respond well to them. Use them liberally!

Yet, children of this age group are also quite literal. And why not? They are rewarded for being literal in school! On a spelling test, one must spell every word correctly to get a 100. Being creative doesn't work! Two plus six is always eight. Giving another answer does not demonstrate creativity as much as it does failure to understand addition. Children are even literal in their rules. If there is a rule, it must be followed exactly, and the consequences for its infraction must be clearly laid out.

So, children of this age are comfortable with a God who is mighty and powerful. They have no problem with God as a rule-giver. They want God to be fair, which frequently means to punish the bad guys and reward the good ones. They also want God to be their best friend, a relationship that is so important. Yet, it is precisely this relationship that can create problems. If a child prays to her best friend, but does not have her prayer answered, she is confused: is God her best friend or not? Her human best friend would do her a favor if she asked or promised to do something for the friend in return. Why doesn't God behave like a best friend?

We might dismiss such questions if the child prays for something trivial or something that takes advantage of another. But, there are poignant prayers for which adult dismissal is inappropriate. What do we say to the child who prays that her parents will stop fighting...but they still do? What do we say to a child who prays that her asthma will get better...but it doesn't? What do we say to a child who prays that his beloved dog will not die...but it does? These prayers are for important things for which many adults would also pray. In such cases, children should be allowed to voice their feelings about God, just as the ancient psalmist did. We are called to listen and reflect with them, not judge them.

## Major Phases Beginning in Early Elementary School Years

*Fear of looking dumb,*
*not being liked, or being embarrassed*
*Unable to lie*
*and unable to tell truth.*
*He stutters fiercely.*

Most people want to be well liked, and most do not want to be embarrassed in front of others, so this fear is not unusual in human development, but the depth of it might be. Because children want to fit in so much, they really want to be like others. Being unique is not something that they desire at this age. Furthermore, they don't want to say or do anything wrong because they fear what their peers' reaction will be. Parents and teachers need to remind children repeatedly that not everyone needs to be the same and that differences are good. That's why God made so many varieties of everything—bugs, flowers, animals, people! Children can also be reassured that, even though it is hard, they can survive when they make a mistake. It is normal to make mistakes, and everyone makes them every day. Because many young elementary school-age children think that certain adults never make any mistakes, adults can point out to such children the mistakes they have made in the last twenty-four hours to make the point that minor mistakes are not only natural but OK.

*Distaste for opposite sex;*
*crushes on teachers*
*Stare each other down–*
*Stupid is as stupid does.*
*War of words keeps on.*

At this age, boys understand that they will grow up to be men, and girls understand that they will grow up to be women. Be alert to any child who doubts that this is the case, because, at this age, that might be a red flag in terms of gender development. Most children of this age prefer to stay with their own gender or look with suspicion at the other, calling the other "stupid." Because all children can display aggression at this age, there might even be some verbal aggression involved. Although aggression cannot be condoned, the dislike of the opposite gender is part of growing one's identity as either male or female, and it is normal. It will end soon enough!

In spite of this, many children have a "crush" on their teacher, who they idealize as the perfect man or woman. They might even have fantasies of marrying the teacher. In this age group, this too is normal behavior and is only worrisome if (a) a teacher responds inappropriately, such as making the child his or her favorite, making inappropriate physical contact, spending time alone with the child, or excluding other children; (b) the child persists in this belief after he leaves this age; or, (c) the child makes inappropriate sexual or pseudo-sexual contact with the teacher. In such cases, professional help is indicated.

### *"Everybody's doing it."*
*Standing on railing*
*(even though Dad said, "Do not.").*
*"Jump," urges his pals.*

This is usually said by a child who wants to do something that others her age are doing but whose parents will not permit. Although parents can (rightly) point out that everybody isn't doing it, that will probably make no difference to the young person who is trying to use peer pressure on the adult. This is natural since the child is becoming susceptible to peer pressure herself. Adults need to stand their ground, but use empathy: "I know you'd like to do this, and it seems like everyone else is doing it. These are the reasons that I'm not so sure about your doing it. [List reasons.]"

Such behavior also stems from a sense of entitlement at this age: "If others are doing something, I should too, because I've been good" (or "We have the money"). Children need to learn that, in the long run, no one is entitled to anything, but this lesson will not be fully learned until adulthood (if then).

### Procrastinating or "forgetting" chores, homework, and so forth

*Dog miserable*
*boy forgot her food (again)—*
*parents not amused.*

Play *is* more fun than work. Most children who procrastinate or "forget" are simply prioritizing their time according to their own desires. Who can blame them? It's worth a try! Adults need to emphasize that certain things must be done before others and the reasons that this is true.

Many people think that procrastination is due to laziness, but procrastination might be used because a child really doubts that he can do something right or perfectly. So, he puts it off until the very last minute, almost guaranteeing that it won't be done right! In this case, he can say, "If I had had more time, it would have been perfect." Many teens and adults use this same line of reasoning, but it is a flawed one, meant only to protect one from facing the fact that even when one gives a project one's all, it still might be far from perfect. It's important to explore why a child feels the need to procrastinate repeatedly.

"Forgetting" might be intentional or quite unintentional. Some children are so caught up in the moment that they truly are not thinking about what needs to be done in the next hour. For those children, a memory aid—like making a list—might really help.

### Habits

*Nails down to the quick—*
*so, she hides hands from rude stares;*
*after all, they're hers.*

Every human being has some habit, some behavior, that is used when she is bored, anxious, or otherwise stressed. Although toddlers and preschoolers can have habits (for example, sucking a thumb), adults think that children do not need habits as they grow older. That is incorrect. Habits can be quite helpful when a child is stressed, helping him to calm himself. They also can be used to an extreme.

What are some habits seen at this age? Nail-biting, hair-twirling, leg-shaking while sitting, rocking, even nose-picking (although this is more likely to be seen at younger ages). When adults see a child engaging in such behaviors repeatedly, it's important to find out something about what is evoking him or her. What's causing the stress, the anxiety, the fear? Is the child bored? If the underlying cause of the behavior can be elicited, it is much more likely that the behavior itself can be successfully managed.

## Summary • Questions • Resources

Increasingly adept in her physical abilities, the young elementary school-age child turns her attention to mastering the subjects that will help her get along in the world. At the same time, she compares herself to others who do much worse or much better in the classroom. Eager to belong, her best friend is important to her developing concept of self and teaches her not to be selfish. She learns to do the right thing not just to avoid punishment but to please others. If it has been encouraged, her prayer life is rich, for she considers God her constant ally. It is up to adults not to alter that perception, which, unfortunately, will change soon enough.

### Questions—Catechists

- What would be your approach to a shy six-year-old who cannot seem to do anything right?

- What would you say to a parent who criticizes his seven-year-old for being upset with God because of an earthquake that killed thousands?

- How would you manage a situation in which an eight-year-old really does not seem to have any friends in class?

### Questions—Parents

- What would you do if your eight-year-old really believes that everyone else is smarter than he is?

- What would be your approach if your six-year-old still sucks her thumb?

- What would you tell your child if she is upset that his prayers were not answered? How would you help your child keep confidence in God?

## Resources

Erikson, Erik: *Childhood and Society*. New York: WW Norton & Co., 1985 [especially chapter 7].

Fowler, James: *Stages of Faith: The Psychology of Human Development and the Quest for Meaning*. San Francisco: HarperSanFrancisco, 1995 [especially chapter 17].

Kuhmerker, Lisa: *The Kohlberg Legacy for the Helping Professions*. Birmingham, Ala.: R.E.P. Books, 1991 [especially table on pages 28–29].

McMillan, Julia, Catherine DeAngelis, Ralph Feigin, and Joseph Worshaw (eds): *Oski's Pediatrics: Principles and Practices, Third Edition*. Philadelphia: Lippincott Williams & Wilkins, 1999 [especially table 395–1].

Schor, Edward (ed): *(The American Academy of Pediatrics) Caring for Your School-Age Child, Ages 5 to 12*. New York: Bantam Books, 1996. [Excellent reference book.]

Siberry, George, and Robert Iannone (eds): *The Harriet Lane Handbook*. St. Louis: Mosby, 2000 [especially chapter 9].

Singer, Dorothy, and Tracey Revenson: *A Piaget Primer: How a Child Thinks*. New York: New American Library, 1978 [especially chapter 2].

# PRETEEN YEARS

· · · · · ·

*Wants to grow up fast—*
*ten going on twenty-five,*
*will lie about age.*

• • •

*Not really a teen*
*and not still a child either—*
*twelve and hating it.*

They call them the "twixt-and-tween" years. They are not quite teenagers, but they want to be. They are not quite children, but they still act like children more often than not. Welcome to the preteen years, corresponding roughly to ten to twelve years old. Preteens hate the idea that they are still considered children and long to be teens. That's why their speech, likes, dislikes, and activities look more like those of their thirteen-year-old siblings than their eight-year-old siblings. They want to be older, yet often want the advantages of being younger.

## Physical Development—Gross Motor

*Soccer ball a blur*
*to goalie—heart not in game,*
*whose mind somewhere else.*

*Awkwardly rising
on toes, young ballerina
feels seven foot tall.*

Preteens continue to develop strength and coordination in their large muscles. Increasingly, they are able to run faster and play harder than they could at younger ages…but only if they try. Many preteens are already developing a sedentary lifestyle, spending hours watching TV or videos, surfing the net, or playing video games. Individuals who began the discipline of playing a sport or practicing some physical activity are in better shape than those who engage in very few physical activities or only halfheartedly do so. In addition, preteens are growing taller even before the growth spurt that will herald puberty. Girls begin their linear growth spurt at around ten years, while boys begin at twelve years. At this age, many girls might be taller than the boys in their class by several inches. As a rule, the legs grow faster than the arms do, although eventually, body parts will be in proportion to each other.

As early as nine to ten years in girls and ten to eleven years in boys sexual development can begin. The timing of this development is related to heredity and environmental factors, and, perhaps, other unknown factors. Once the brain signals the body to produce growth and sex hormones, the progression of events that lead to a mature male or female body has begun. The full process—from the earliest signs to the end of sexual development—takes between four and five years.

In girls, breast buds appear a bit before underarm and

pubic hair. This is because the enlarging and maturing ovaries are releasing estrogen and progesterone, the female sex hormones. As the girl matures, she will become "rounder" and more shapely, with curves at the breast line, waist, and hips. All of these external changes reflect internal changes in a girl's ovaries and uterus.

In boys, the penis begins to lengthen, and the scrotum enlarges and becomes coarser in appearance. Scant pubic, underarm, or facial hair might also begin to be seen, although chest hair does not appear until much later. A young man's voice may begin to deepen as his larynx becomes larger and his vocal cords lengthen, but the quality of that voice change is erratic with "cracking" of the voice which is a common (and embarrassing) occurrence. Boys of this age might begin to experience wet dreams, ejaculation of semen at night. In the beginning, the semen has very few sperm, although that will change as the boy matures. These changes are all related to the fact that the boy's testes and adrenal glands are making testosterone, the male sex hormone.

Sexual development that begins much earlier than that of similarly aged peers generally causes embarrassment, with attempts to conceal any development that might be noticeable to onlookers.

The average age of menarche (the first menstrual period) in U.S. girls is about 12.4 years, but it can occur anytime from age ten to fifteen. The average age at which a boy first produces viable sperm is about a year later, but can occur at any time from ages eleven to fifteen. All of this means that it is possible for two preteens to have intercourse and some girls to become pregnant.

## Physical Development—Fine Motor

*Writing atrocious—*
*doesn't care; far too busy*
*with video games.*

• • •

*First necklace a joke—*
*Strung the beads unevenly.*
*Lots better next time.*

For both groups of young people, fine-motor skills generally improve toward adult levels. Preteens are developing greater hand-eye coordination and steadier hands. Their fingers are also growing longer. That means they are better able to print and write legibly than they were in the past. If they engage in hobbies that challenge their dexterity or hand-eye coordination, their skills are likely to improve over their baseline and compared to those similarly aged preteens who have no such hobbies.

## Physical Development— Sleep, Diet, and Elimination

Preteens usually need eight to ten hours of sleep each night. They do not always appreciate that fact, so when they stay up late, they are usually tired the next day.

Usually preteens (especially boys) have a great appetite, as they are eating for their increased level of growth. Increased intake is to be expected, but because too many calories ingested (versus calories expended) can lead to being overweight or obese, preteens should be encouraged to engage in as much physical activity as they can. The foods that most preteens prefer are usually the most caloric.

Most preteens have established their own normal elimination pattern, which is usually one formed bowel movement every day or every other day, and three to six urinations each day, depending on the amount of fluid ingested.

## Psychological/Emotional Development

*Unexpectedly*
*shy about wearing braces—*
*she looks in mirror.*

• • •

*Will wear wrinkled clothes*
*forever if allowed to;*
*he's too cool for words.*

Preteens want to be teenagers in the worst way! And so, the once compliant child now has become (at least occasionally) a demanding, moody young person who is beginning to believe that her parents know nothing. She might be embarrassed to be seen with her parents and may criticize their clothes, music, politics, and beliefs. In other words, nothing they do is right. This behavior will continue at least through early adolescence and maybe longer. It seems to be more marked in girls, although boys certainly display the behavior also.

The preteen might balk at clothes selected by a parent and wear clothing that seems, well, odd to the parent's taste.

She might grumble about her parents being the meanest parents in the world because they will not let her go out or stay up late. "You're ruining my life!" she might dramatically announce. She is usually exaggerating. "Everyone else is doing it" is another claim that can easily be disproved if the parents have enough energy, which they frequently do not. While a preteen wants to be different, she does not want to be *too* different from her peers.

All of this is related to the Eriksonian stage *identity vs. role diffusion*, a stage that will last throughout most of adolescence. Although this stage can begin in the preteen years, it is a little less marked in them compared with young adolescents because preteens usually have less independence, mobility, and street smarts.

What's this stage all about? When a child was younger, he understood he had no power. Only big people had power, money, cars, and so on. So, the child had no problem aligning himself with parents and other adults as a way to share some of that power or prestige. In other words, it was great being someone's son. As he gets older, however, he wants power for himself. It is not enough to be someone else's child. He wants to be his own person.

To do that, he needs to know who he is, independent of his parents. In fact, he begins to try to distance himself markedly from his parents' ways, looking for interests that are, in some cases, completely opposite of theirs. He is likely to try different roles (friends, hobbies, courses of study, or sports) to find out who he really is. This is normal behavior as long as the exploration does not lead to illegal or immoral actions, which, unfortunately, it sometimes does.

Preteens really enjoy their friends and love to talk on the phone and e-mail one another...for hours. They do not understand the dangers of Internet chatrooms and the predators who might be masquerading as another teen. When their parents try to warn them about this danger, they might think their parents are ridiculous. This is especially true if the teen *has* lived a relatively sheltered life, with no real harm occurring to anyone she knows. Her lived experience speaks against bad people trying to hurt her.

## Cognitive Development

*Mind like a steel trap—*
*wanting to know everything*
*reading all the time.*

• • •

*Homework still undone*
*at ten o'clock at night! Ha!*
*Can't go to bed yet.*

Emerging from a period of relative certainty about the world, almost everything was either right or wrong, preteens enter a world where issues are not so simple. There are gray areas to every issue, and preteens can find this disconcerting even as it is liberating. Part of their dismay is that for several years, they were *so* certain—about their beliefs, practices, and rules. Now, they're not so sure. As they meet more and more people who are not like them, they are exposed to other viewpoints, which might be radically different from those of their families. As they have experiences that their parents would not even have dreamed of at this age, they can see for themselves that things are not always the way they were presented. Admittedly, parents present the world to younger children in a certain way so that they will not be frightened or confused. For the rapidly maturing young person, her parents' actions seem to demonstrate less kindness and more deception or simple ignorance.

Preteens continue in their ability to master academic subjects, notably those in which they have a personal interest. Although their thought processes are maturing in terms of being able to start to think abstractly, they can still think in a very concrete fashion. In spite of what they hope, they are still not at the level of adult thinking. That will more fully blossom in adolescence.

## Social Development

*Ready, dimpled grin*
*a magnet for girls his age—*
*he's not yet aware.*

• • •

*Not yet discovered*
*the joys of opposite sex;*
*she prefers reading.*

Boys prefer friends with whom they can do favorite activities. Girls prefer friends with whom they can share their innermost thoughts. Most boys are uncomfortable talking about personal feelings, but they want to be a part of something larger than themselves. So, there might be a group of boys who enjoy not only their time playing sports together but also their time together discussing sports or collecting sports memorabilia.

On the other hand, most girls welcome discussions about feelings. That is why many preteen girls love to talk for hours on the telephone. They can never get enough of talking about themselves and others. Children of this age begin the habit of gossiping. Early in the age, they might only gossip about people whom they admire, but as time goes on, they will also engage in gossiping about those whom they do not like or whom they are ridiculing. Whether the gossip has a basis in reality or not, it is unkind, and young people should be called on it.

Although girls and boys are starting to notice and take a greater interest in one another, most preteens are not interested in dating or pairing off with someone of the opposite sex.

Mixed groups of girls and boys are just starting to be tried, and there might be a great deal of embarrassment unless there is an outside reason that the young people are gathered together, such as working together on a service project. Being in a group is a safe way to approach the opposite sex, having friends there for support. In the safety of the group, they can experiment with flirting or catching the attention of someone of the opposite sex surrounded by their friends who understand them and can support their efforts. Keep in mind that some preteens are very much like younger children and have absolutely *no* interest in members of the opposite sex. At this age, this should not be a concern.

## Moral Development

*Grounded yet again;*
*made not an honest mistake—*
*has happened before.*

• • •

*She tries not to look*
*at poor people on the street—*
*makes her feel guilty.*

Although preteens might still be doing the right thing in order to serve their own needs or to please others, another factor comes into play: the importance of their friends and their groups. In fact, both preteens and young adolescents look to their group for support in their decisions and ways to handle situations. In Kohlberg's third stage, a young person might do something (that they consider "right") if it helps others, especially if they are members of one's "group," even if doing so would break an external law. This stage can be overemphasized if young people see the adults in their lives "bending the rules" to suit the interests of members of their own group. This stage demonstrates the rising importance of relationships in the young person's life.

An example or two will illustrate the implications of this stage. Two boys are close friends. One asks the other if he can *copy* the other's homework, because he did not get around to doing it. The assignment was to have been done on one's own, without any help from others, and that was made clear when the assignment was given. Because they are friends, the first boy agrees to share his work. The next day in class, the teacher says, "Now, sign your name at the bottom of your work to show that you worked alone on this assignment and did not help anyone else." The two boys sign their names without guilt. After all, they are friends, and what they did is not hurting anyone else.

Or, take another example. Two girls are shopping. The first girl holds her finger up to her lips as if to say, "Shhhh!" She then slips a lipstick into her pocket. The second girl knows stealing is wrong (as did the first girl, given her action), but says nothing and accompanies her friend outside. "Made it!" says the first girl triumphantly. "I don't think you should have done that," says the second girl. At that moment, a security guard approaches both girls and tells the first that another customer saw her take something. The first girl denies it and runs away. When he asks the second girl if her friend took anything, she says, "No." Even though she knows that shoplifting is wrong, she could get her friend into a lot of trouble if she tells the truth. So, lying does not seem so wrong in this case. Anyway, the store has lots of lipsticks and lots of money. What difference is one little lipstick going to make in the end?

Although standing up for one's friend is good, standing up to the truth might be *the* right thing to do. Adults working with preteens can devise their own scenarios and ask the opinions of the young people and why they think that way. In this way, in a safe situation, such young people can "think out loud" and hear what others have to say (including the adult) and why they say it. They can also strategize ways to handle such situations if they should occur in their own lives.

## Spiritual Development

*And why didn't God*
*fix it so no one would cry?*
*A much better plan.*

• • •

*Praying and smiling:*
*"Thank you, God, for making me*
*(almost) all grownup."*

In the preteen and young teen years, Fowler noted that children are moving away from the literalness of younger years and are beginning to see the complexities of living. When they were younger, everything was so "cut and dried"; certainty was never an issue.

Now, these young people see a different world. Few things are certain. People have many different opinions about a lot of things, even in matters of faith. When they were younger, they did not encounter too many people who held beliefs vastly different than those held by their family. Now, they are meeting all kinds of people with many different beliefs or values. Who's right?

Fowler called the faith stage *synthetic-conventional*. Synthesis means "to make something, to bring a number of things together to make something new." The conventional is the usual, the expected. So, preteens have one foot in their previous life (the conventional) and one foot in their present life (synthetic).

As they are learning about the many beliefs that people have, they begin to try to bring them together in a way that makes some sense. No longer is it sufficient to say that the only good people are those with a particular type of belief, because the preteen can see many people with vastly different beliefs or values acting in good ways, such as helping the poor. So, the young person needs to make room for differences of opinion.

Yet, it *was* nice when everything was so predictable, so certain. So the preteen hangs onto some affiliation with that part of his past. In terms of faith, he holds onto a certain allegiance to his old parochial school or his parish. "We've got the best school in the whole city," he might say with pride. "Our pastor is the best," she might brag. "I can't imagine not being Catholic (or Lutheran, Presbyterian, Methodist, Episcopalian, Baptist, and so on)." Yet, she still wonders what makes all these faith traditions different from one another.

Perhaps the most difficult aspect of this stage is when she sees people of the *same* denomination have such different views. One would expect that people of different denominations have varied beliefs. But in the same faith tradition? How can that be? This is particularly confusing when the preteen remembers that just a couple of years ago, everything in his faith tradition seemed so certain. This is what one had to believe. So, what makes a Catholic a Catholic, or a Baptist a Baptist? Although adults know the major tenets of their faith tradition, they, too, might have a hard time listing, say, the top five beliefs. There might be some variation, as some people wouldn't insist on someone else's number four but would bring in another tenet that others did not even list.

This is highlighted, especially at this age and the next, by the issue of whether one *really* must attend church every weekend. For some families, this is their belief. It must be done unless one is ill. For other families, their belief is that church is good to attend, but not necessary. One can be a good person without regular church attendance.

An example is in order to illustrate the problem: Two friends of the same faith tradition live next door to each other. One's parents never permit her to miss Sunday worship, except for illness. The other's parents feel that charity is more important than church attendance. They have no problem with missing church for a variety of reasons. The two girls are having a sleepover on a Saturday. Earlier in the day, they volunteered at the local soup kitchen because that is what the second set of parents do one Saturday each month. Toward bedtime, the first girl asks what time they will be getting up for church in the morning. The second girl says, "We don't go to church every week. Do you?" "Yes," says the first girl, "My parents say it's wrong not to." "Well," says the second, "nothing bad has ever happened to us. Anyway, my folks say you don't have to go to church to be good." The first girl is confused. She can see that her friend's parents are good people. Her own family never helps at the soup kitchen, but they attend church every Sunday. What is the right thing to do? What does the faith tradition say is right?

## Major Phases Beginning in Preteen Years

*"I'm almost an adult!"*

*"I am not a child,"*
*she says fifty times a day:*
*who's not yet convinced?*

As mentioned earlier, preteens want to be all grownup in the worst way. They even round their ages upward! So, when they want to do something that their parents feel they are too young to do, a common response is, "I'm not a child. I'm almost an adult." Alas, wishing does not make it so. Adults need to be both sympathetic and empathetic, and try to remember when they were young and trying to be older. They also need to be clear in their explanations as to why the young person is too young to do whatever it is that she wanted to do. The young person might not like it, but at least, she will know the rationale behind the decision.

*"You can't make me!"*

*What's a mom to do?*
*The boy towers over her,*
*and he's only twelve.*

This is related to the above phase, expect in this case, the young person does not want to do something that the adult wants him to do. The implication is that since the young person is no longer a child, the adult cannot compel him to do whatever the adult wants. As mentioned above, adults need to be both sympathetic and empathetic, and try to remember when they were young and yearning to be older. They also need to be clear in their explanations as to why it is appropriate for the young person to do whatever it is that the adult requested. The young person still might not like it, but at least, he will know the rationale behind the decision.

### Procrastination ("forgetting")

*"Oh, I'll get to it."*
*Ain't no way! T'would be a first.*
*Mind too much like sieve.*

This was discussed previously. The same psychological dynamics might be being played out, only on different issues.

### Disrespect to parents ("sassing")

*Her sassing and smirks*
*make it clear to the whole mall—*
*her parents are jerks.*

As the preteen becomes older, it occurs to her that her parents (or teachers) do not have all the answers. In fact, they might just be wrong about certain things. In some preteens' minds, if the parents (or teachers) are wrong about certain things, maybe they're wrong about *everything*. This insight gives some preteens license to be rude to adults. Rudeness is not to be tolerated, especially rudeness in public. A way of handling this is to speak with the young person about how she would feel if the parent (or teacher) publically humiliated her. Why would such behavior be wrong? Preteens are now old enough to experience the "shoe on the other foot," as part of the beginning of their development of empathy and abstract thought.

### Using bad language
*To show off, he cursed.*
*Satisfied, he cursed again.*
*Too bad! He liked it.*

Many preteens see adults curse. Some of these adults are in their own homes. When they were younger, they might have been told that they were too young to say such words if they tried to do so. Well, now, they are older! Many preteens will try a few choice words so that it can make them feel grownup. Bad language is inappropriate for preteens. One might point out that such words are usually only one syllable...for good reason. They are words meant to express a sudden emotion. Clearly, the young person can think of other words or ways to describe what she is experiencing, and, if she really can't, the adult might be able to help. Cursing is simply sloppy expressive language and although adults do it more than children, there is really nothing mature about it. In fact, the way some adults curse, it's almost as if they are having a temper tantrum!

## Summary • Questions • Resources

As his physical and intellectual skills become fine-tuned, the preteen realizes that he is no longer a little child. He is almost a teenager, frequently rounding his age upward so that he does not seem so young. He likes to be in a group of friends, who can have a lot to say about what he likes or does not like. He might even do the wrong thing if it will help out one of his friends. He might begin to sass adults in authority and even to use bad language, especially if it will get him what he wants. He no longer accepts simple answers about the world or about religion and God. In fact, he might begin to have some serious doubts about some of what he has been taught in religion class or heard in church. His prayer life might be filled with a number of questions to God as well as petitions. He looks to those older than him for examples to follow. Adults do well to set the best example they can and encourage his questions or expression of his doubts.

### *Questions—Catechists*

- What would you say to a ten-year-old who questioned the need for church attendance on Sunday?

- How would you manage a situation in which an eleven-year-old uses "bad" language just to get his classmates to laugh?

- What would you say to a twelve-year-old who believes that standing up for one's friend is more important than following any rules or laws?

## Questions—Parents

- What would be a good approach to take when your twelve-year-old says, "I'm not a child anymore"?

- What would you say to your ten-year-old who does not want you around...ever?

- How would you explain sexual predators on the Internet to your trusting, friendly eleven-year-old daughter?

## Resources

Erikson, Erik: *Childhood and Society*. New York: WW Norton & Co., 1985 [especially chapter 7].

Fowler, James: *Stages of Faith: The Psychology of Human Development and the Quest for Meaning*. San Francisco: HarperSanFrancisco, 1995 [especially chapter 18].

Kuhmerker, Lisa: *The Kohlberg Legacy for the Helping Professions*. Birmingham, Ala.: R.E.P. Books, 1991 [especially table on pages 28–29].

Schor, Edward (ed): *(The American Academy of Pediatrics) Caring for Your School-Age Child, Ages 5 to 12*. New York: Bantam Books, 1996. [Excellent reference book.]

Siberry, George, and Robert Iannone (eds): *The Harriet Lane Handbook*. St. Louis: Mosby, 2000 [especially chapter 9].

Singer, Dorothy, and Tracey Revenson: *A Piaget Primer: How a Child Thinks*. New York: New American Library, 1978 [especially chapter 2].

# YOUNG ADOLESCENTS

· · · · · ·

*Adolescence rough—*
*things changing too rapidly.*
*She longs for childhood.*

· · ·

*Getting to the age*
*where he needs to shave—awesome!*
*Thinks he looks rugged.*

Clearly no longer children, young adolescents can see the light at the end of their tunnel in terms of growing up. Compared to preteens, they have greater freedom, more responsibility, and more opportunities outside their home. They can engage in abstract thought more easily than they could just a couple of years earlier. Their bodies are maturing, and some of them might have already reached their adult stature and are showing secondary sex characteristics. They are gaining a greater interest in the opposite sex, and they are seriously thinking about their future in terms of colleges, careers, and so forth. But, they are not mini-adults. They are still young people who are not quite at adult levels of maturity in various aspects.

In many cases, their developmental stages look very much like those of their preteen counterparts. The difference is that young adolescents are further along the stages that preteens are just beginning. That makes a great deal of difference, since some young adolescents are already moving toward older adolescence in certain areas of development.

## Physical Development—Gross Motor

*Dunking the big shot*
*right at the (final) buzzer—*
*thrill of victory!*

• • •

*Why the big feet and*
*why the long legs but short arms?*
*Way too weird for words.*

Much of what was said about preteens applies also to young adolescents, except that many will have experienced a growth spurt of four or more inches in a relatively short time. Such a relatively large change in height (and perhaps also weight) can make young adolescents feel ill at ease in their bodies, and they might seem clumsier than they were previously, as they trip over their newly large feet. With time, they will adjust to their more mature bodies.

With increased height and weight, especially in boys, comes increased muscle mass and corresponding strength and dexterity. Many adolescent boys tower over their parents...and can eat them out of house and home! Whereas in elementary school, girls might be as strong as boys, as boys mature, that clearly is no longer the case since boys' muscles are larger than those of girls. Naturally, there are always exceptions, and there can be wide variations in the degree of physical development, even among young people of the same age. Some young adolescents have a negative body image because their development is far ahead or far behind that of their friends or because they do not have the body they want. This is more common in girls than in boys and can contribute to a heightened self-consciousness.

Sexual maturity is progressing along, as most of the girls will have had their first menstrual period, even if cycles are irregular. Some girls will have attained adult height and adult sexual development. Young adolescent boys are still developing adult sexual characteristics. Some boys at this age need to shave, while others have barely a wisp of beard. Some boys of this age have experienced a deepening of their voices, while others still have the higher pitched voice of their preteen years. Wet dreams are common.

For a more detailed explanation of pubertal changes, see the corresponding section on physical growth in the chapter "Preteens Years."

## Physical Development—Fine Motor

*Hands a bit shaky*
*as apply the eyeliner*
*to quivering lids.*

• • •

*Bleeding fingers and*
*callused hands demand a break!*
*Guitarist plays on.*

For both groups of young people, fine-motor skills generally continue to improve toward adult levels, because of ever-improving hand-eye coordination, dexterity, and growth of fingers. Handwriting, especially in girls, becomes neater. Hobbies that require fine-motor skills help to improve those skills, so practice means that the young artist draws better, the young guitarist plays better, the young jewelry maker becomes more proficient. The fine-motor skills of girls might improve if they begin to apply makeup.

Generally, young people get better at that which holds their interest, so that is part of the key for the young person: to find something that will really capture his interest and dedicate himself to it.

## Physical Development— Sleep, Diet, and Elimination

Young adolescents usually need eight to twelve hours of sleep each night. As with younger children, shortchanging themselves on their amount of sleep to stay up late does not help their performance the following day.

Usually young teens (especially boys) have a great appetite, as they are eating for their growth spurt. So, increased intake is to be expected, but because too many calories ingested (versus calories expended) can lead to being overweight or obese, young teens should be encouraged to engage in as much physical activity as they can. The foods that most teens prefer are usually the most caloric. For a discussion of a fear of being overweight, see the section "Major Phases Beginning in Preteen Years" in the previous chapter.

## Psychological/Emotional Development

*She hates her freckles—*
*mean boys call her "Spotted Sue";*
*she avoids mirrors.*

• • •

*Didn't make the team—*
*horrendous blow to ego.*
*Angry tears erupt.*

If preteens want to be teens, then teens want to be adults. With their greater independence and mobility, young adolescents can encounter novel situations, places, and things that they never would have encountered when they were kept closer to home. Experiencing these new things can make a young teen feel grownup. It can also mean trouble if a teen is poorly prepared for them. This is especially true for situations or people connected with alcohol, drugs, sex, or illegal activities.

Young teens have a sense of invincibility. "It won't happen to me" is the mantra. They think of themselves as too smart to be fooled into doing something stupid or too healthy to be hurt by any abuses of their bodies. Unfortunately, they are wrong.

Young adolescents' emotions seem to "roller-coaster," as they are up one minute and down the next. At one moment, they insist they are all grownup. In the next instant, they want to be held. At another moment, they seem sullen or indifferent. At the next minute, they are enthusiastic and engaged. All of these are parts of an adolescent's personality, and she must come to terms with the presence of them all.

## Cognitive Development

*Hard-pressed to explain*
*report card with grade of F—*
*can only stutter.*

• • •

*Aced another test!*
*Others look on with envy*
*and she doesn't care.*

Piaget called the stage of adult thinking that adolescents are learning *formal operations*. Prior to adolescence, an elementary school-age child requires tangible objects and real-life experiences to think about certain issues. In the preteen years, this starts to shift toward more abstract thought. In adolescence, abstract thought becomes easier, and one is beginning the process of being able to imagine oneself in a situation that one has never been in before (and might never be in). One can consider a variety of possibilities, not only the obvious or what has been personally experienced.

For example, an elementary school-age child would have difficulty in writing an essay about homelessness because she has nothing to base it on, unless, of course, she has been homeless. When she is fourteen years old, she might be able to produce a magnificent essay on the topic. Why? At fourteen, she can synthesize her knowledge of the topic (gleaned by research) with her own beliefs and feelings so that she can imagine what homelessness would mean for her. She can empathize with those facing that situation, placing herself in their place. Her essay reveals an integration of the facts and the experiences, something impossible at a younger age.

Young teens who are interested in school continue to increase their knowledge base, as they find some subjects to their liking and others not. Their ability to learn new information and to synthesize it into what they already know seems endless for those who are motivated to learn and who receive support for their motivation from their families. Young teens who are not motivated to learn school subjects are frequently motivated to learn other material outside school. There are many causes for a lack of motivation, and among the most important are a lack of support from family and friends, and a belief that learning something will not make a difference in one's life. A lack of motivation might also be a cover for insecurity about one's abilities.

## Social Development

*Chatting into night*
*on phone to one she has seen*
*all day long in school.*

• • •

*Reading far too much*
*into smiles of such cute boys;*
*she makes wedding plans.*

Friendships continue, and young people tend to "hang" with others of their own age and gender. But, unlike the preteen years, there is a greater interest in the opposite sex. So, mixed groups are more common, and young people are finding it fun to be around others of the opposite sex. A few might be shy about this, and that is normal behavior. Mixed groups permit one to try out one's personality with the opposite sex with members of one's own sex there for support. Many girls have learned to flirt from the safety of a group of other girls. Many boys have learned how to approach girls from the safety of his best pals.

Although girls and boys are starting to notice one another more and take a greater interest in one another, most young adolescents are still are not interested in dating or pairing off with someone of the opposite sex. Some young adolescents are very much like younger children and have absolutely *no* interest in members of the opposite sex. At this age, this should not be a concern. At the opposite extreme, a few adolescents are very interested in the opposite sex, and might even experiment sexually. This is not the norm.

One's peer group is important, and it is *usually* comprised of those who share similar interests, opinions, and standards, but not always. Because no adolescent wants to be left out, a teen might go along with the crowd, against his better judgment. Sometimes, it almost seems as if a young teen would hide a part of himself just to fit in. For example, if the crowd thinks it's not cool to ace a test, the smartest teen might try to do well but not *too* well so that he will fit in with the crowd. It's as if his intellectual gifts are embarrassing him, so much that he will deny that they exist in the way that they do. All of this is related to a certain lack of confidence, an uneasiness, about the way he is and whether anyone will like him the way he is.

## Moral Development

*Yes, it was quite wrong*
*to steal another's answers.*
*But no one got hurt.*

• • •

*Always sticking up*
*for all her friends, even though*
*they don't do the same.*

As with preteens, although young adolescents might still be doing the right thing in order to serve their own needs or to please others, the importance of their friends and their groups might be having a major impact at this age. In fact, both preteens and young adolescents look to their group for support in their decisions and ways to handle situations. In Kohlberg's third stage, a young person might do something (that they consider "right") if it helps others, especially if they are members of one's "group," even if doing so would break an external law. This stage can be overemphasized if young people see the adults in their lives "bending the rules" to suit the interests of members of *their* own group.

For a greater discussion of this age, see the corresponding section under "Preteen Years."

## Spiritual Development

*Why must she attend*
*church with hypocrites when she*
*can pray much later?*

*So, what is the deal—*
*what do I gotta believe*
*to get to heaven?*

A continuation of Fowler's *synthetic-conventional* stage with even greater levels of synthesis being attempted because a young adolescent's experience is greater than that of a preteen. She naturally comes into greater contact with other people, especially those who are different. In addition, her greater ability to think in an abstract way means that she is having an easier time placing herself in someone else's place than she ever could have done as a preteen. She is better able to see that every story has two sides, every issue has at least two viewpoints. All this means that her ability to synthesize is increasing, while her desire to remain "conventional" is decreasing, unless the peer group to which she belongs is conventional. For a greater discussion of this topic, see the corresponding section under "Preteens Years."

## Major Phases Beginning in Young Adolescents

A number of the phases discussed in the section under "Preteen Years" are still operant at this age as well and should be reviewed. Some additional ones follow.

### Invincibility
*Wouldn't have believed*
*that world could change so quickly—*
*car crash wake-up call.*

Young adolescents believe that nothing bad will happen to them. Because they are usually in good physical condition, they believe that they are not at risk for illnesses, injuries, or negative consequences of sexual activity, smoking, alcohol, and drug use. They believe that they are too smart (see below) to do anything stupid, to get caught, to get into trouble, or to get hurt.

In one way, a sense of invincibility is wonderful, because it means that the young person is probably not anxious or tentative in his overtures to the world. On the other hand, a sense of invincibility can get a young person into serious trouble if he gets too cocky and takes foolish risks. Although boys are more likely to demonstrate this behavior than are girls, both genders are affected.

Although we would not want adolescents to lose their zest for life or their physical health, we do want them to be realistic. So, it is good to discuss the way of the world with them, not in a preachy sort of way but in an honest manner, allowing lots of time for questions, impressions, and suggestions for how situations or people can be handled.

*"I'm too smart for that"*
*Trusting much too much*
*in resources not mature,*
*his mind races on.*

This statement is directly related to the one preceding, and is a reflection of the young person's sense of invincibility. In other words, "Bad things happen to others because they're not as smart or as aware as I am. Because I am smart and aware, I will be protected from bad stuff or people." Oh that it would be that easy! Plenty of smart people have been seriously injured in car crashes; become terminally ill; gotten hooked on drugs, cigarettes, or booze; or been arrested. It takes only a momentary lapse in judgment to create many years of problems and sorrow.

So, we do want to emphasize that young people *do* need to be smart and aware—aware that the dangers are real and can happen to anyone. Adults do not need to "scare" young adolescents, but they need to be realistic in their discussions about the bad things that can happen. Such adults do well to avoid being perceived as sarcastic, rude, angry, or condescending in their discussions about many matters with teens, for if teens perceive any of these attitudes, they will not be able to really hear what these adults are saying—no matter how right it is.

### Experimentation with alcohol, tobacco, drugs, sex

*'Twas only one time—*
*would never have done it more.*
*Got burned just the same.*

Some young adolescents experiment with sex, tobacco, alcohol, or drugs as an attempt to fit in with an admired crowd that endorses such experimentation. Other young adolescents do so because they are trying to rebel against parents, test their limits, or are simply curious. Still others experiment because they are sad or lonely, and they believe that these substances or behaviors will alleviate their bad feelings.

Many adolescents believe the word on the street: adults do not want kids to engage in such behaviors because they do not want teens to have fun. They reason, "I bet the adults did all this stuff when they were kids, so why can't we?"

The reason for the experimentation must be sought so that help might be offered. Yet, regardless of the reasons for experimentation, young adolescents need to know the truth about all these activities. Each of these activities can have serious, even deadly, consequences. The best person to discuss these matters should be the young person's parent, but sometimes a parent smokes or drinks to excess herself, limiting her credibility. Or, a divorced father has numerous "sleepover" girlfriends. How can his son believe him if he talks about the dangers of sex at a young age? In the absence of a credible parent, teachers can discuss these matters, or they can bring in a doctor or other respected authority figure. Many times, the best speaker is a young adult who has been "burned" by the very behaviors that the young adolescents want to try. This is especially true if this young man or woman has a connection to the group, such as a member of the same church, graduate of the same school, resident of the same neighborhood. The more like the young adolescents this speaker is, the more likely they are to listen to him or her.

### Questions whether God exists
*Looking at the mess*
*of this old world all around—*
*doubting that God is.*

In their early adolescent years, some adolescents question whether God exists. Maybe they've seen a program on TV or read an article about God's existence. Maybe they've heard others talk. No matter the source, young people themselves start to ask questions about evil in the world and why God doesn't stop it. As one fourteen-year-old said, "I see all the bad stuff, and, if I were God, I'd want it to all go away. If God is powerful, God could make it go away. If God loves us like everyone says he does, he'd want it to go away. But the bad stuff is still here. So, you gotta wonder, 'Is there really a God out there?'"

As with many other developmental tasks in this age group, permitting open discussions about God, the presence of evil in the world, and the degree to which free will is involved can start many young adolescents thinking seriously about the big issues rather than reacting to them. As we can see from Scripture, God is not angered by questions, even from the prophets and psalmists. Otherwise they would have been eliminated before they could even have written a word! Review these parts of Scripture and share them with young people.

## Summary • Questions • Resources

As her physical and intellectual skills are rapidly maturing, the young adolescent looks increasingly to her peer group for "norms" of behavior—what's in and what's out. This might cause problems if she does the wrong thing simply to please members of her group. As the attraction to the opposite sex increases, she might spend more and more time in front of the mirror, voicing her dissatisfaction with her perfectly wonderful appearance. Her opinion of herself is usually not entirely accurate, as one day she thinks that she is an ugly failure (she isn't) and the next day she thinks that nothing can happen to her because she's too smart (she's wrong). She might seriously question the religion of her heritage, especially if she sees significant adults acting in hypocritical ways. Fully aware of the media and others' opinions, she wonders if there even is a God. Looking at the world, she cannot tell if there is. Adults in her life are called to show her God's presence in their words and actions.

## Questions—Catechists

- A few students in the ninth-grade confirmation class say that they don't really believe in God. What would you say?

- What would you say to a thirteen-year-old boy who says that sex with lots of people must be good because that's what his dad does? Would you speak to his father as well?

- How would you impress upon a group of eighth-graders the dangers inherent in Internet chatrooms?

## Questions—Parents

- What would be your approach if you found your fourteen-year-old son on an Internet porn site?

- What would you say to your fifteen-year-old daughter whose response to every piece of parental advice is, "Don't worry. I'm too smart for that?"

- What would be your approach if your thirteen-year-old son has no friends and prefers to be alone?

### Resources

Erikson, Erik: *Childhood and Society.* New York: WW Norton & Co., 1985 [especially chapter 7].

Fowler, James: *Stages of Faith: The Psychology of Human Development and the Quest for Meaning.* San Francisco: HarperSanFrancisco, 1995 [especially chapter 18].

Kuhmerker, Lisa: *The Kohlberg Legacy for the Helping Professions.* Birmingham, Ala.: R.E.P. Books, 1991 [especially table on pages 28–29].

Pruitt, David (ed): *Your Adolescent: Emotional, Behavioral, and Cognitive Development from Early Adolescence through the Teen Years.* New York: HarperResource, 2000 [especially chapter 1]. [Excellent reference book.]

Siberry, George, and Robert Iannone (eds): *The Harriet Lane Handbook.* St. Louis: Mosby, 2000 [especially chapter 9].

Singer, Dorothy, and Tracey Revenson: *A Piaget Primer: How a Child Thinks.* New York: New American Library, 1978 [especially chapter 2].

# OLDER ADOLESCENTS
• • • • • •

*Rejected (again)*
*by still another girlfriend—*
*what is he lacking?*

• • •

*Poring and poring*
*over college catalogs—*
*Too many to choose.*

O lder adolescents are almost adults, although, many
times, they act like much younger children. Their con-
cerns are more about adult matters than those of even young
adolescents. They are thinking about their future—what college they will attend and/or what profession they will take
up. They are wondering about what kind of life partner
they want and also what kind of life partner they will be.
They probably have at least a part-time job and are learning to manage their money, finally understanding how hard
it can be to make ends meet.

## Physical Development—Gross Motor
*Once hated long legs—*
*now not so bad. Rest of her*
*finally caught up.*

*Another bucket!*
*Towers over opponents.*
*A man of stature.*

In the later adolescent years, most teens will have reached their adult height, although some male adolescents might grow in height until they are twenty to twenty-one years old. Older adolescents have adult bodies. Physically, these young people are generally in great physical shape, their strength and endurance near lifetime peak levels, which usually occurs in the young-adult years. This is especially true if the young person plays a sport or exercises regularly. This is also a reason that older adolescents can stay up all night to play or to study: they simply have great endurance and energy, if they have been taking care of themselves. In terms of sexual function, adolescent males are near their peak sexual function, while it will be years before the adolescent girls reach their peak. That is why it seems that boys of this age are always ready for sex and girls are not. Overall, over 50 percent of fifteen- to nineteen-year-old adolescents have had sexual (genital) relations. The percentage who have tried oral sex might be even higher.

## Physical Development—Fine Motor

*Loves calligraphy—*
*smiles approvingly at her*
*handcrafted note cards.*

• • •

*Practicing often,*
*perfecting magical tricks*
*to amaze young kids.*

Although finger growth has ceased, hand-eye coordination and dexterity can still improve, especially if the older adolescent practices her skills. This ability of fine-motor capacities to become sharper can continue for a number of years if one works at it. Obviously, fine-motor skill is more important in some jobs and professions than in others. As has been stated earlier, usually if one wants to improve in this area, works at it, and is rewarded in some way for it, improvement occurs.

## Physical Development— Sleep, Diet, and Elimination

Older adolescents usually need eight to ten hours of sleep each night. As with younger teens, shortchanging themselves on their amount of sleep to stay up late does them no favors in terms of their performance the following day.

Older adolescents have good appetites and, ideally, have a good sense of what they should and should not eat, and the proper amounts. They have their preferences and their dislikes, and they are usually great fans of soda and fast food.

As for weight consciousness, see the discussion under "Major Phases Beginning in the Preteen Years" chapter. As adolescents become older, many become even more fixated with their appearance than they were when they were younger, and so the problems of unrealistic weight expectations might not necessarily disappear.

Although urinary elimination patterns might vary by the amount of fluid ingested, bowel elimination patterns are generally fairly routine.

## Psychological/Emotional Development

*Not another zit!*
*Not on prom night! It can't be.*
*Everyone will laugh.*

• • •

*Likes to stay up late—*
*best things happen late at night.*
*He'd outlaw mornings.*

Older adolescents are coming to the end of the Eriksonian stage of *identity vs. role diffusion*. Hence, many (but not all) older adolescents have a clear idea of who they are, what's important to them, and what they want to do with their lives. Naturally, this is a lifelong process, but older adolescents are well on their way. Because of their definite ideas about many issues, they can be quite assertive about what they believe, even if it is at odds with what their family believes.

In fact, many older adolescents have had a period of questioning every parental rule or suggestion, which underscores that parents are no longer in control of their teens. Some adolescents have rebelled in various ways, and a few might still be rebelling, even in their older adolescent years. This is all a part of forging one's own identity, which began in the toddler years. The adolescent wants to be taken seriously as a person in her own right, one who has well-reasoned ideas and beliefs. Although she might love her family dearly, she is not her family, and she wants the world to know that.

As long as parental-adolescent disagreements are over relatively minor issues (curfew, makeup), there is probably no cause for concern, while other, more serious issues, such as drinking or drug use, would be and might require professional help. Above all, adolescents need their parents' love and support. They need to know that their parents will be there for them, no matter what. If a parent and his adolescent have had good communication over the years, it usually does not end with adolescence but, instead, deepens. Parents who have been able to communicate well with their children all along (and, more importantly, listen well) are more likely to be respected and listened to by their children—and vice versa.

Most older adolescents have a self-esteem that is actually higher than what they had at a younger age, mostly because they are more comfortable with themselves. If they have been developing in a healthy manner, they like their bodies and their abilities, and they accept their flaws as well. They are understanding that everyone has flaws and everyone makes mistakes. These need not be devastating in terms of a person's self-image. They certainly can learn this lesson from loving, but flawed, parents. In addition, greater self-esteem might be related to the fact that older adolescents are more independent, perhaps even earning their own money to buy things that they need or want.

## Cognitive Development

*Last-minute pressure—*
*science project a real drag*
*for her, the artist.*

• • •

*Late for school again—*
*neither a morning person*
*nor a school person.*

Well into Jean Piaget's stage of formal operations, most older adolescents can grasp abstract concepts as well as many adults. They also are able to understand and follow more complex logical arguments. These two abilities mean that the older adolescent is able to think about many things that she had not previously pondered, and she can see both pros and cons (and their subtleties) of many issues, even though she *is* attracted to one side or the other because she is her own person.

Some of what the older adolescent thinks about is the future, especially his own. What will the world be like in twenty years? Will I get married? Will I be able to find a good job? Where would I like to live? These are no longer random questions born of daydreams, but the organized questions of one who is personally invested in their answers. As in their younger years, older adolescents benefit from healthy adults role models to whom they can voice their questions (and possible answers) aloud. Ideally, that is a parent, but it also might be a teacher or neighbor.

Most older adolescents are eager to learn at least a little about a number of things. Such enthusiasm should be encouraged and tapped. This means that, if they are motivated, older adolescents have a phenomenal ability to carry a heavy course load in school and learn a new hobby as well.

## Social Development

*Uh-oh: a slow dance—*
*where to put his hands? Not where*
*he most wants them put.*

• • •

*Hiking up her skirt*
*so she'll fit in with her gang—*
*then her dad appears.*

Older adolescents have several good friends and usually one "best" friend. They like to socialize with their friends in mixed small or large groups, engaging in activities that are fun or that serve others. Adolescents like to be with their friends because they believe (rightly) that their friends understand them better than their parents do. For that reason, they might have an easier time accepting advice from a peer than from their own parents, even when the advice is the same. That is why it is so important for an adolescent to surround herself with peers with wholesome values. This is true even if the peers are, on the surface, not at all like one another. Older adolescents are appreciating that not everyone needs to look or dress alike, a good lesson in tolerance. It is still true that most teens surround themselves with people who are like them. It can be very worrisome when, in an effort to be more popular, a teen tries to "reinvent" herself to fit in with beliefs and interests of a group of which she desperately wants to be a member.

By the older adolescents years, interest in the opposite sex is high, most young people have begun to date. Sometimes a couple does activities with another couple, so that it really is a small group rather than individual dating.

In some ways, dating teaches lessons similar to that of having a best friend: reciprocity, loyalty, trust, sharing of dreams, and regrets. In addition, dating can be great fun if two well-matched individuals enjoy each other. That is the up side. On the down side, dating, like intimate friendships, helps one to learn about how to handle disagreements, rejection, or breakups. These are hard but very valuable lessons to learn. Unfortunately, some adolescent girls also learn about date rape or abuse at the hands of a boyfriend.

## Moral Development

*Invulnerable—*
*that's what he feels when driving*
*eighty miles an hour.*

• • •

*Such a hangover!*
*Head pounding so forcefully*
*her eyes can't see straight.*

Because of their improved ability to think abstractly and to weigh both sides of a debate, older adolescents are better prepared to realize that many factors go into making moral decisions than they were at a younger age. No longer is fear of punishment or need to please others an acceptable reason for doing the right thing. Many adolescents have moved into Kohlberg's fourth stage: *doing the right thing to keep one's group or even society moving smoothly.* So, even if he does not like a societal law, he might observe it because he can see its importance. For example, even though he would like to drive faster than 25 mph in a residential area, he will obey the law because he knows that the neighborhood has many young children in it who have a tendency to dart in front of cars. Driving at the slower speed means he might have a better chance to avoid hurting someone. Or, even though he would like to get a CD for which he has no money, he will obey the law against shoplifting, because he knows that if everyone shoplifted, nothing would be left, and prices would soar, even for him.

Yet, not all societal laws seem just or even there to protect people. In fact, some seem blatantly unfair—only there to protect the interests of a few. For example, an adolescent might believe that capital punishment is applied to minorities or the poor more frequently than it is to wealthy white criminals. The older adolescent will argue against such public policies, saying, in effect, just because something is a law does not mean that it is the most moral way of acting. He will argue most vociferously with his own parents when they act in ways that he considers morally questionable, such as speeding or lying, even if the reason for such behavior seems, on the surface, to be sound.

Although some of this reflects an adolescent's sense of idealism, most are trying to find their own voice, one which is not necessarily the same as that of his parents. For those reasons, older adolescents need the most moral of role models they can encounter, so that they can better understand that taking a point of view opposite to one's parent is not necessarily a moral thing to do in and of itself, as the parents' actions might be moral. Availability of positive, outside role models will highlight this.

## Spiritual Development

*Lotus position*
*new for a cradle Christian—*
*exploring new faiths.*

• • •

*Feeling a bit odd*
*in a Jewish synagogue—*
*girlfriend squeezes hand.*

The Fowlerian stage for older adolescents is called *individ-uative-reflective*. A young person must come to grips with what *she* believes. It is no longer sufficient that her parents believe in a certain way. The stage is individual, because who can determine what one believes except the person herself? It is reflective because much inner work is necessary. In terms of belief in God, a young person of this age might explore other religions in order to see if any belief system is more in keeping with hers. She might cease attending church altogether as she struggles to understand how the condition of the world jives with the notion of a good and loving God. She might espouse atheism or agnosticism as she searches for proof of God's existence in this troubled world.

This stage might take many years to successfully complete, and, it should be noted, some adults have never successfully negotiated this stage. The stage might be quite painful, especially for someone whose faith had been important in her younger years. That is why it is so important to have someone with whom an adolescent can discuss these issues. Although it would be nice if it were the parent, parents might not always be the best persons. They have a vested interest in the outcome, and some parents might feel that their child is rejecting everything that they have given them when they reject parental faith. This belief might make parents very defensive and closed to true communication. That is why it might be easier for a teacher or other trusted adult to discuss these matters; they do not have the emotional attachment to their resolution that parents naturally have.

## Major Phases Beginning in Older Adolescents

Some of the phases listed under "Young Adolescents" continue in this stage as well. In addition, there are several others.

> ### "You don't understand."
> ### (AKA, "You're out of it.")
> *Has to admit it:*
> *not cut out to study law;*
> *dreads telling his dad.*

This is usually said when a young person feels that she is in love or wants to do something of which the parents disapprove. It can also be tied to the idea that parents have forgotten what it was like to be young or do not really understand what the current world is like for a young person. Maybe the adult really does not understand the young person's point. That is why good communication is essential.

Adolescents need limits and rules that have been mutually decided upon. They need to be treated and listened to with respect, so that the adult really understands their position—even if the adult still disagrees with it. There is no place for condescension, anger, or a "know-it-all" attitude, on either side. Above all, teens need adults who care about them.

*"I need my space." I need my privacy."*
*"I need to move out."*
*Living in a room*
*ten by fourteen feet, really*
*needs her private space.*

In the older adolescent years, the need for privacy that started many years before becomes more acute, as the young person does *not* want to spend every waking moment with the family, even though he might love them. He needs his own space—to decorate as he likes, to keep as messy (or as tidy) as he likes, to consider his very own. The need for independence from not only parental rules but also parental eyes is strong. Freedom is calling him! If he cannot get the privacy at home, he might opt to move in with friends. He wants to be on his own. He wants to be his own man. (As an aside, he will not be able to understand his older sibling who wants to move *back* to the family home, say, after a failed marriage.) Parents need to provide as much privacy as is feasible to their nearly-adult children, given the living arrangements with which they must work.

*"I'm not your little girl (or boy) anymore."*
*Parents try hugging*
*nearly-grown son who'd rather*
*a handshake instead.*

The baby is all grown. The youngest in the family is now in college. Just as young people need to adjust to their new adult identities, so, too, do their parents. Although it is natural for parents to wax on rhapsodically about his cute way of waddling when he took his first steps or the terrible diaper rash she had and how her parents had to let her run around naked to clear it up, young adults don't want to hear about it—not yet. Maybe sometime in the future but not now. Hearing those stories is a throwback to a different time, and young adults don't want to live in the past. The solution? Parents need to balance stories from the past with insights about the present and dreams about the future, all the while permitting the young adult to offer their insights and dreams...and questions. In that way, the parent-child relationship can grow throughout life.

## Summary • Questions • Resources

No longer a child, the older adolescent is heading off into the beginning of his adult life. With the crazy situation of the world, it's a little scary. Although, in many ways, he is at the peak of his physical powers, at times, he might wonder if that can get him through it all. Suppose no one will marry him? Suppose he cannot ever find a job that he will really like? Although groups are important, he usually prefers to touch base with a single person, either a buddy or a girlfriend to bounce ideas. He still might think that he is invincible, but he has an increasing sense of the bad things that can happen to people of all ages. He might be conservative in his approach to rules...unless he himself has to be bound by them; then, he might be much more liberal! He searches for what he truly believes in, exploring other religious traditions. He has so many questions, so many issues. Adults do well to provide a listening ear and thoughtful responses to the questions he poses to them.

### Questions—Catechists

- What would you say to a seventeen-year-old who asks why Christianity is better than any other religion?

- How would you respond to a group of high-school seniors who ask you what *you* disagree with in your religion?

- What would be your response to a sixteen-year-old (you've known since first grade) who tells you, "You just don't understand"?

### Questions—Parents

- What is your response when your eighteen-year-old rejects one of your cherished beliefs? Which belief would it hurt the most for her to reject?

- What is your reaction when your seventeen-year-old repeatedly tells you, "You just don't get it, do you?"

- What is your approach when you really do not like one of your son's friends or his girlfriend?

## Resources

Erikson, Erik: *Childhood and Society*. New York: WW Norton & Co., 1985 [especially chapter 7].

Fowler, James: *Stages of Faith: The Psychology of Human Development and the Quest for Meaning*. San Francisco: HarperSanFrancisco, 1995 [especially chapter 18].

Kuhmerker, Lisa: *The Kohlberg Legacy for the Helping Professions*. Birmingham, Ala: R.E.P. Books, 1991 [especially table on pages 28–29].

Pruitt David (ed): *Your Adolescent: Emotional, Behavioral, and Cognitive Development from Early Adolescence through the Teen Years*. New York: HarperResource, 2000 [especially chapters 2 and 3]. [Excellent reference book.]

Siberry, George and Robert Iannone (eds): *The Harriet Lane Handbook*. St. Louis: Mosby, 2000 [especially chapter 9].

Singer, Dorothy and Tracey Revenson: *A Piaget Primer: How a Child Thinks*. New York: New American Library, 1978 [especially chapter 2].